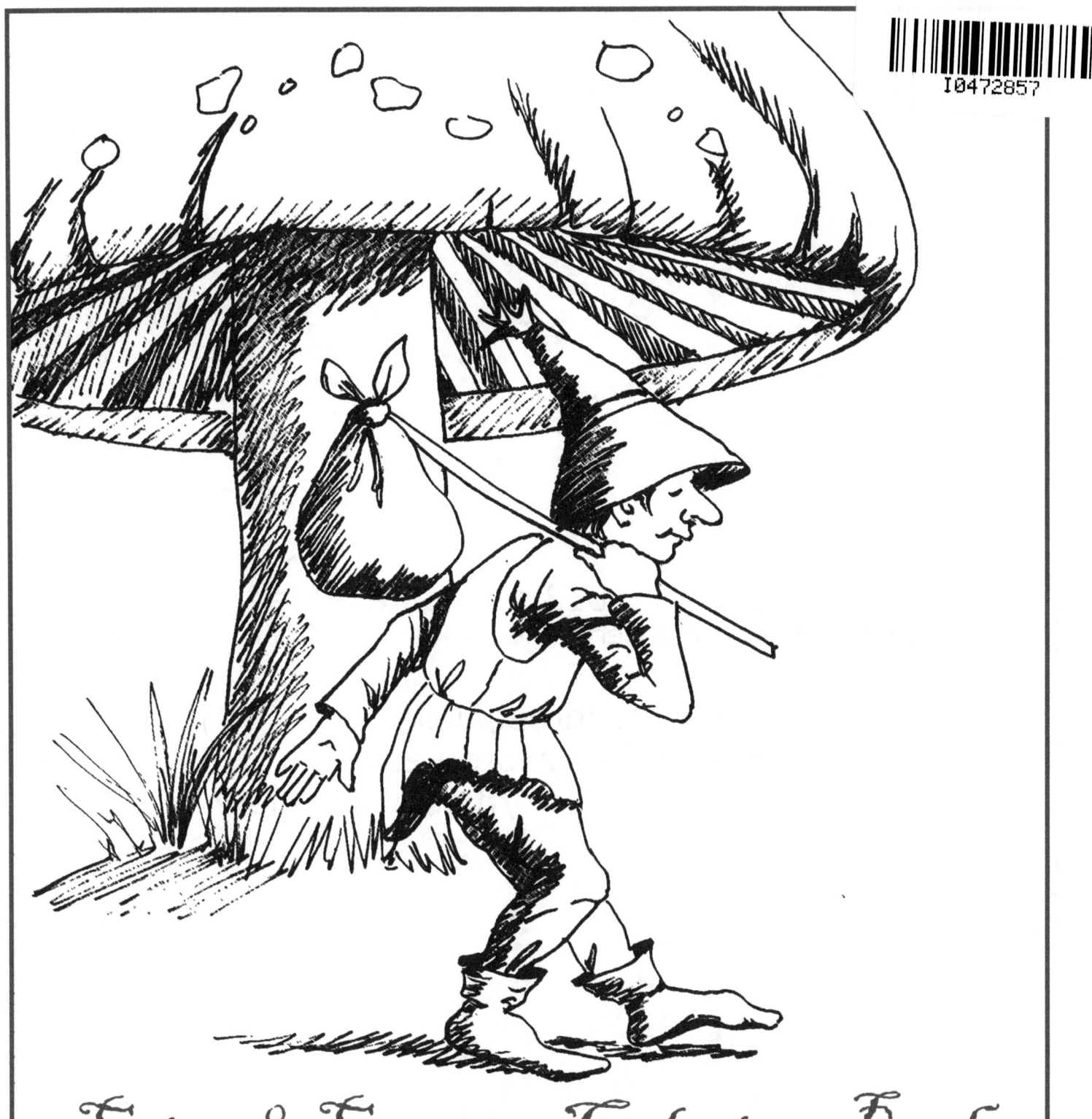

Fairy & Fantasy Coloring Book

by

Ann Gates Fiser

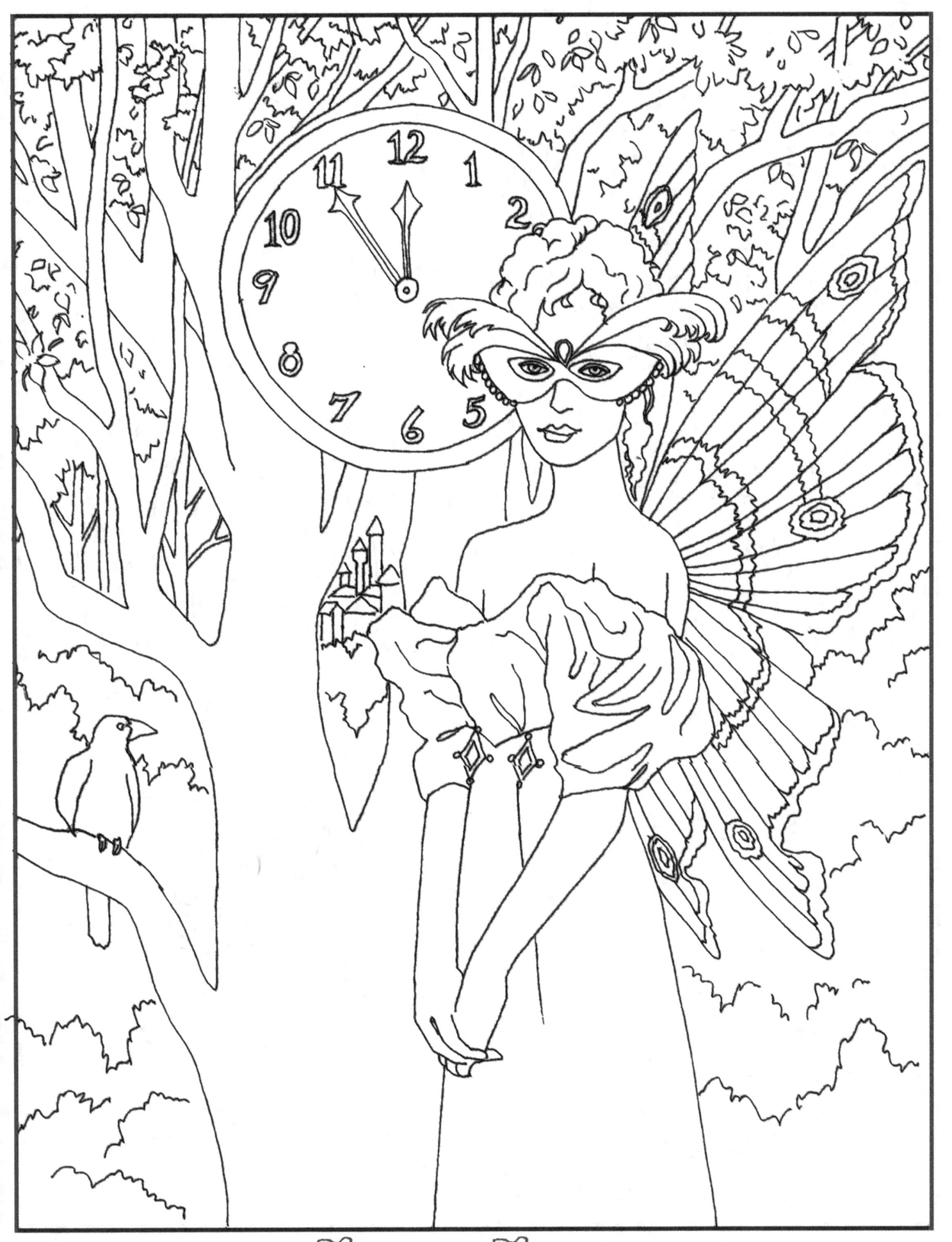

Midnight Masquerade

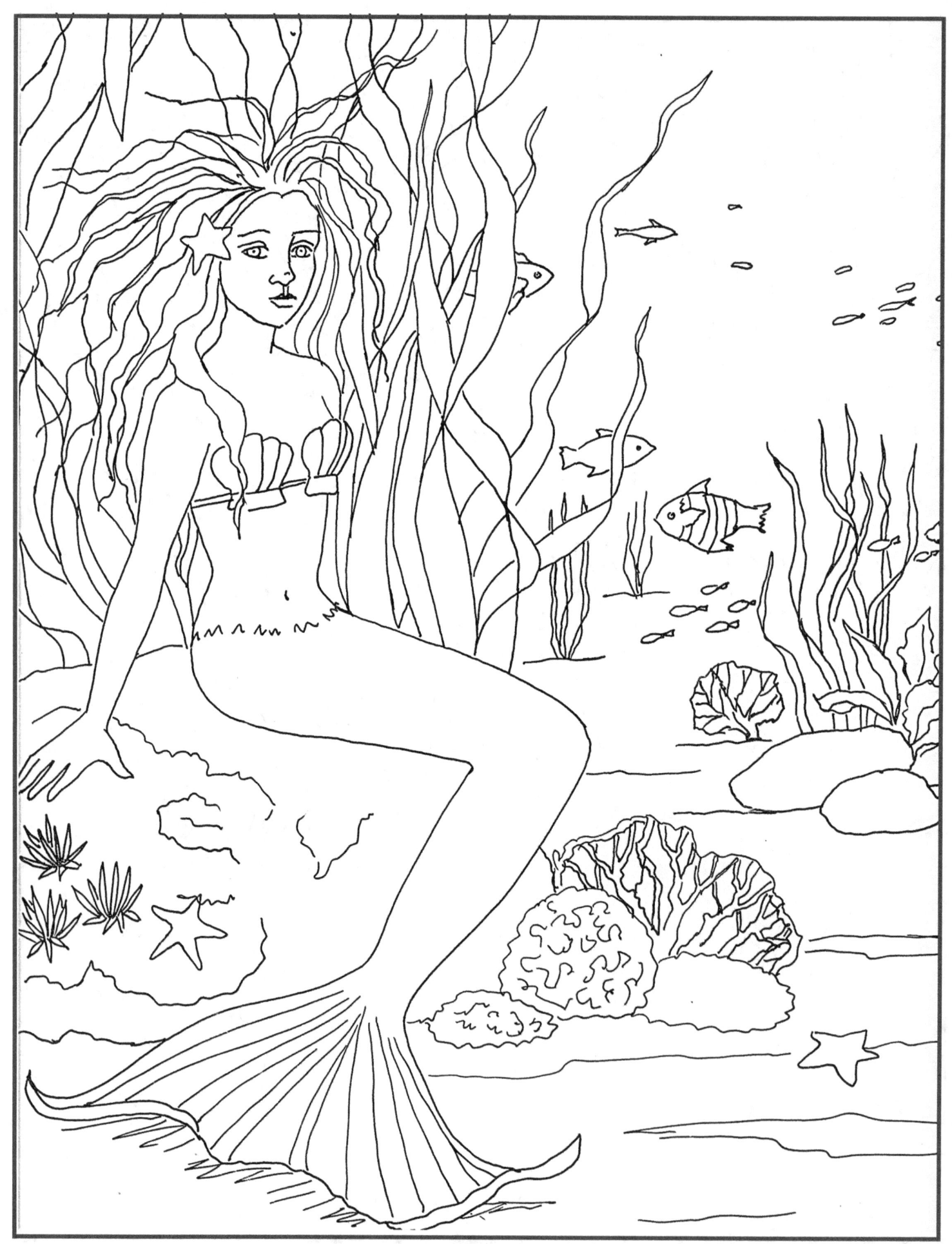

Evia

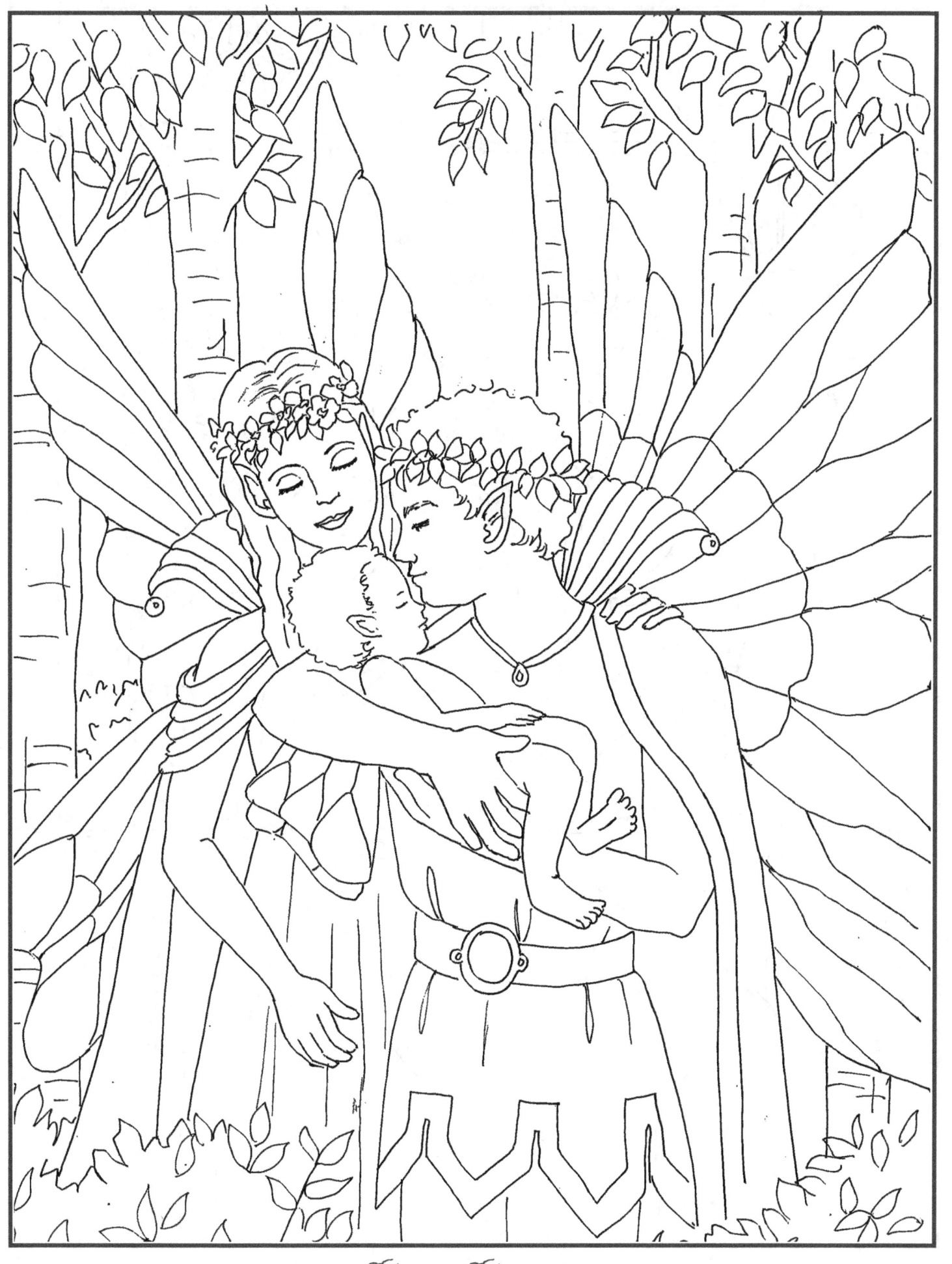

Fairy Family

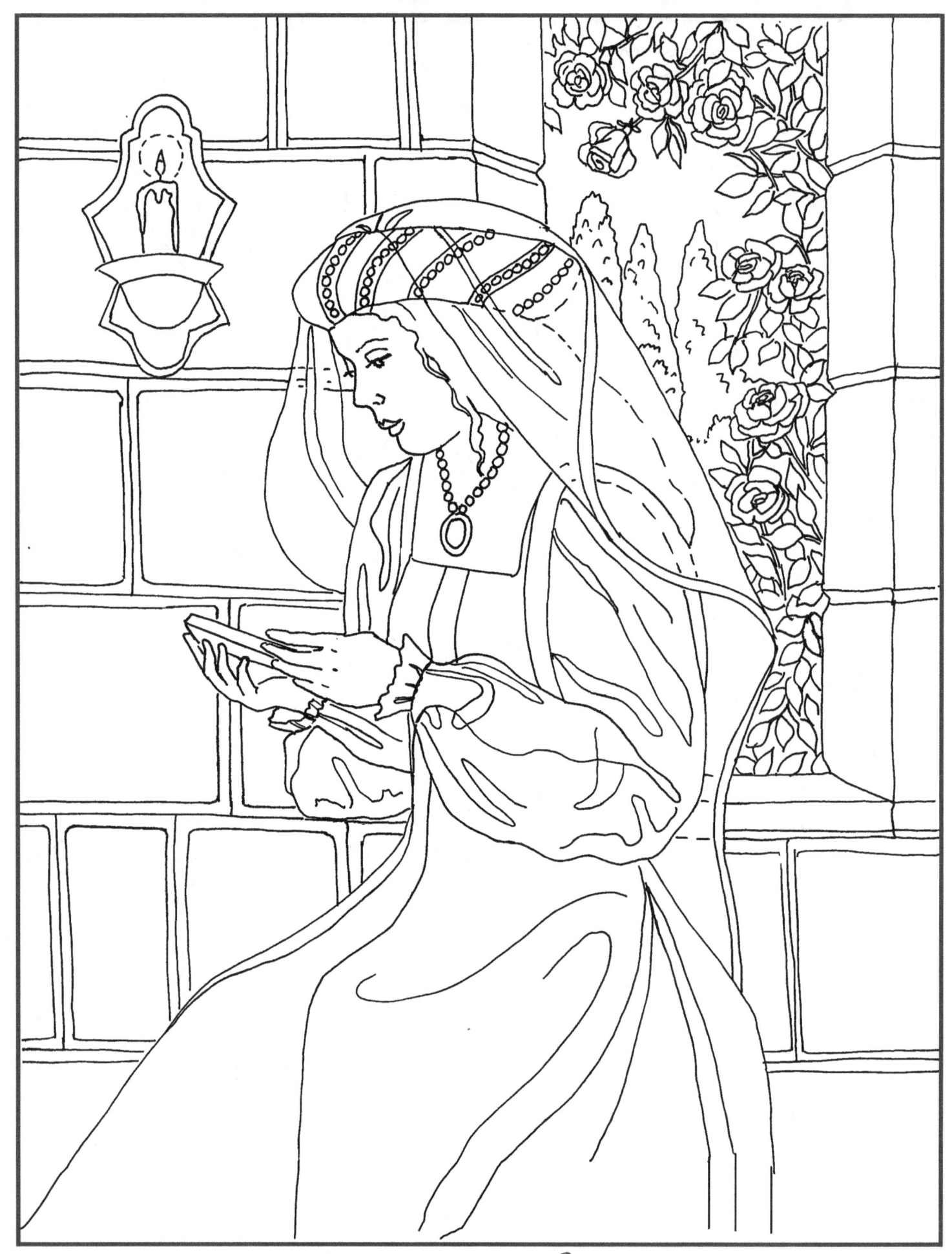

Remembering His Face

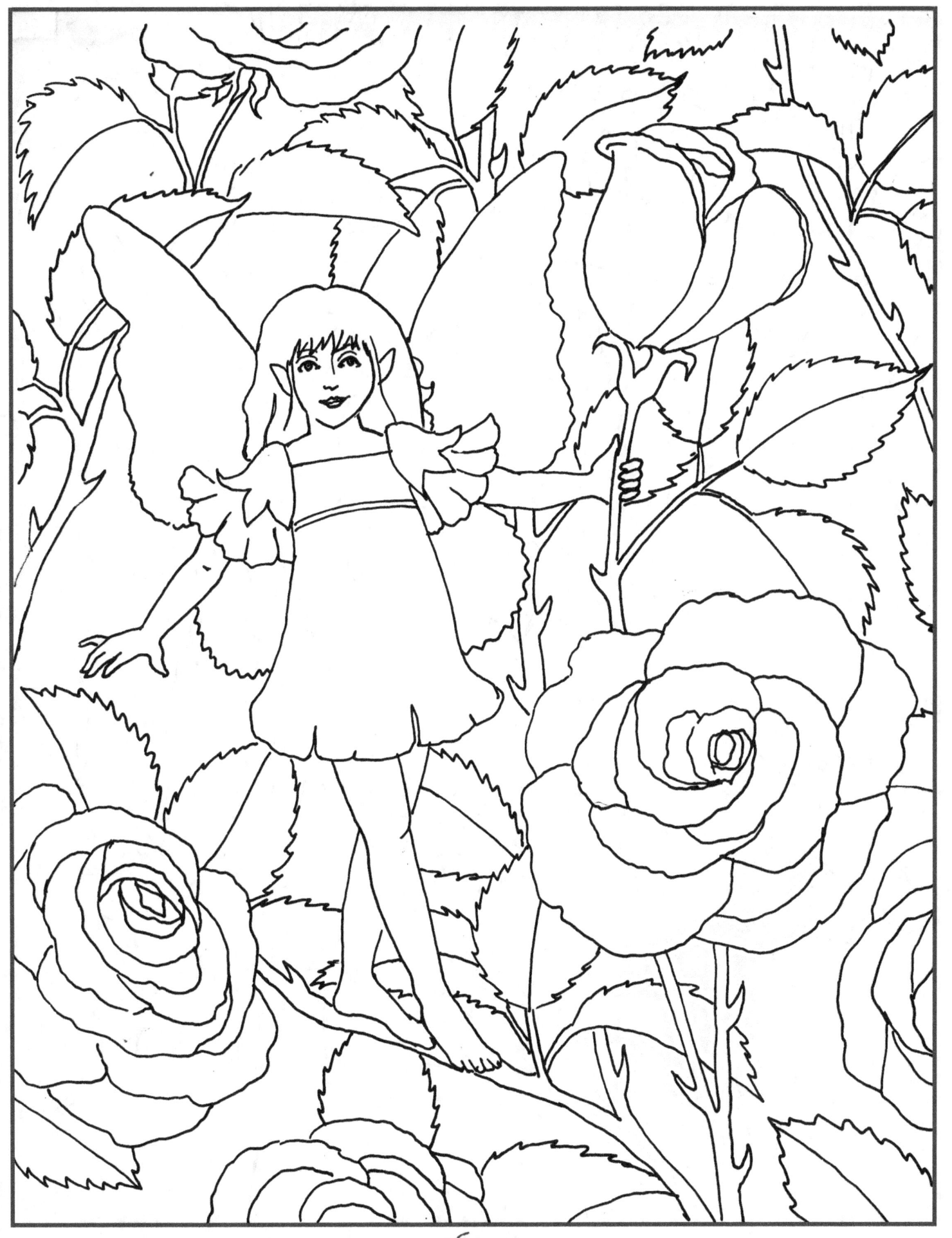

Rose

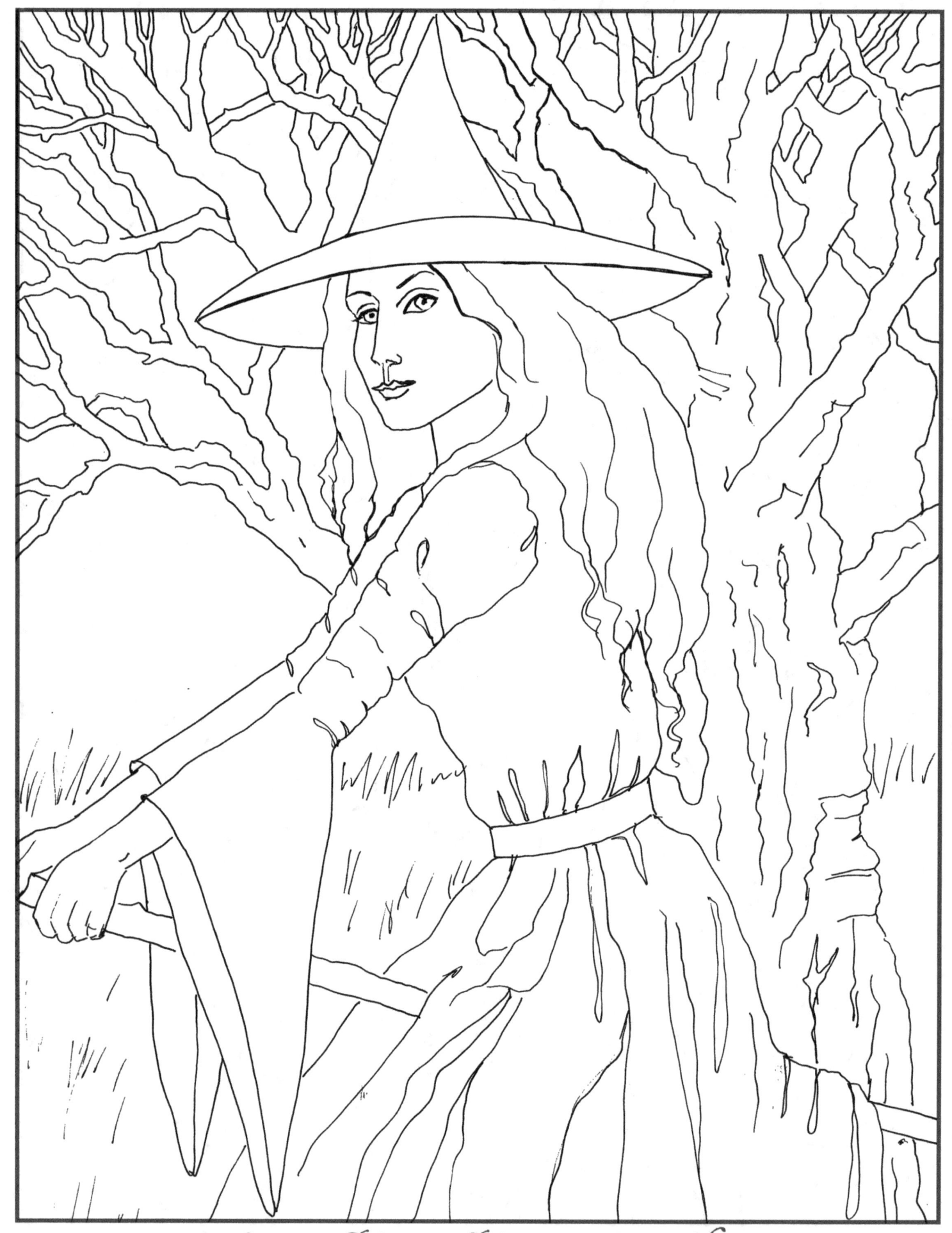

Witches Aren't Always Old Hags

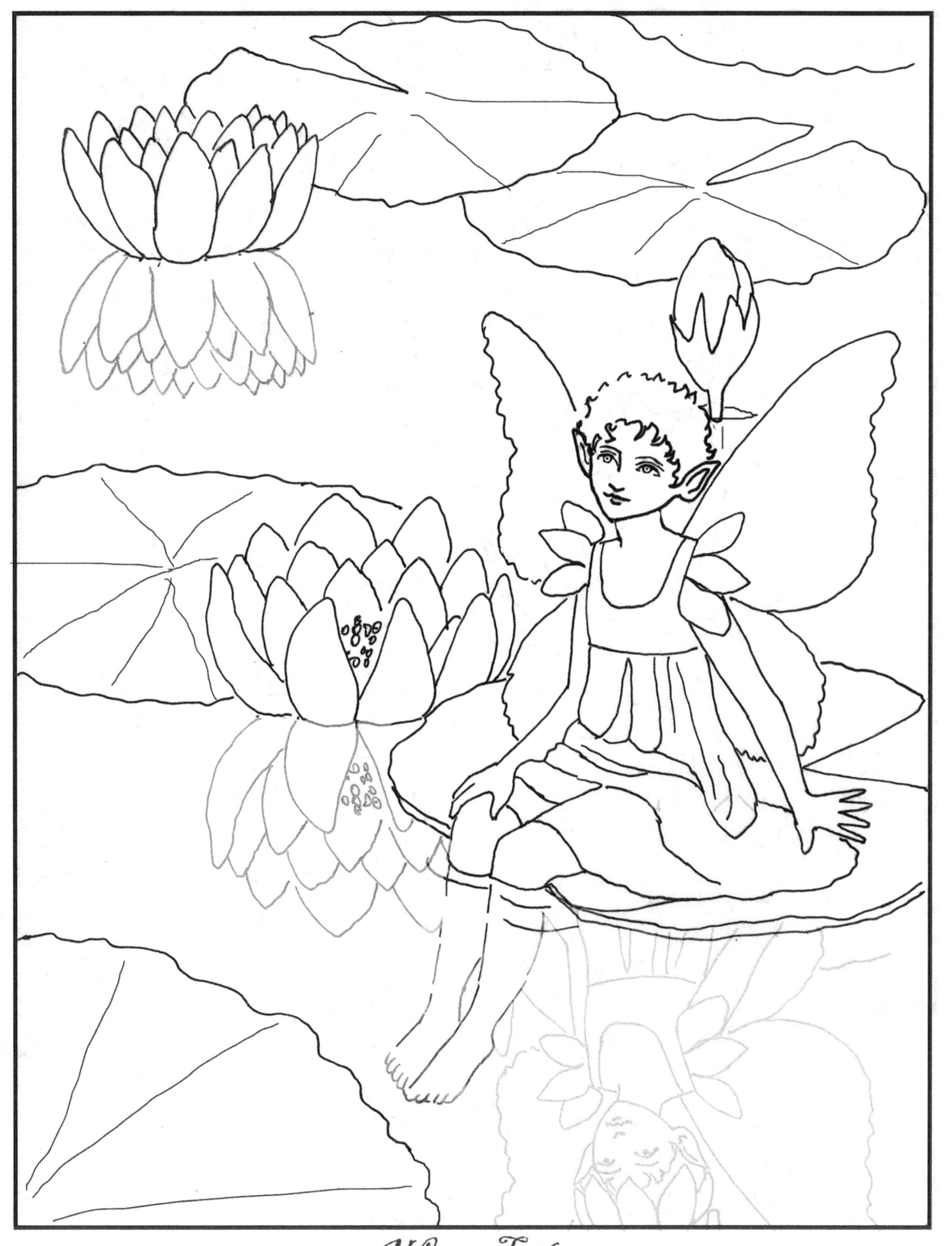

Water Lily

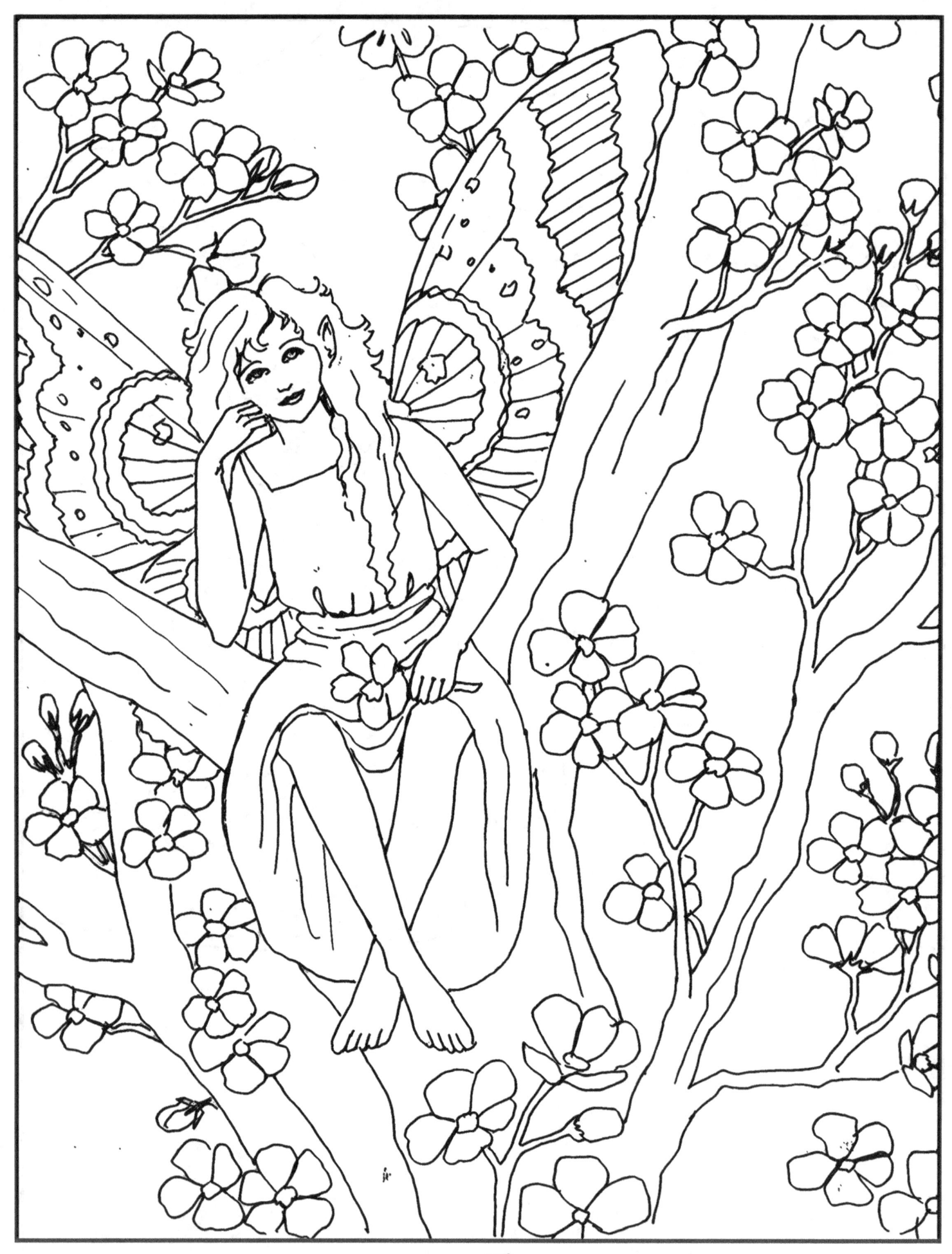

Cherry Blossom

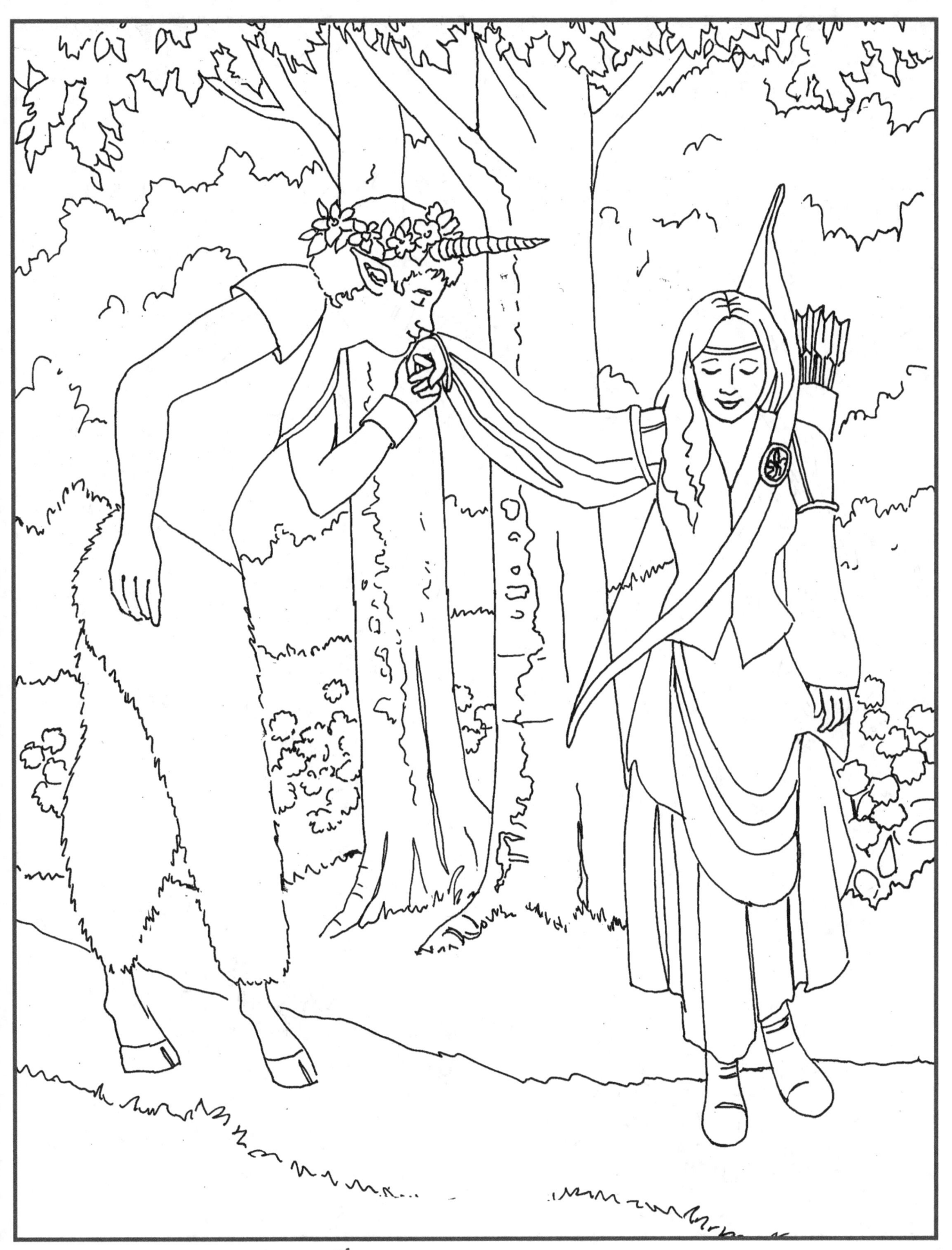

Diana and the Satyr

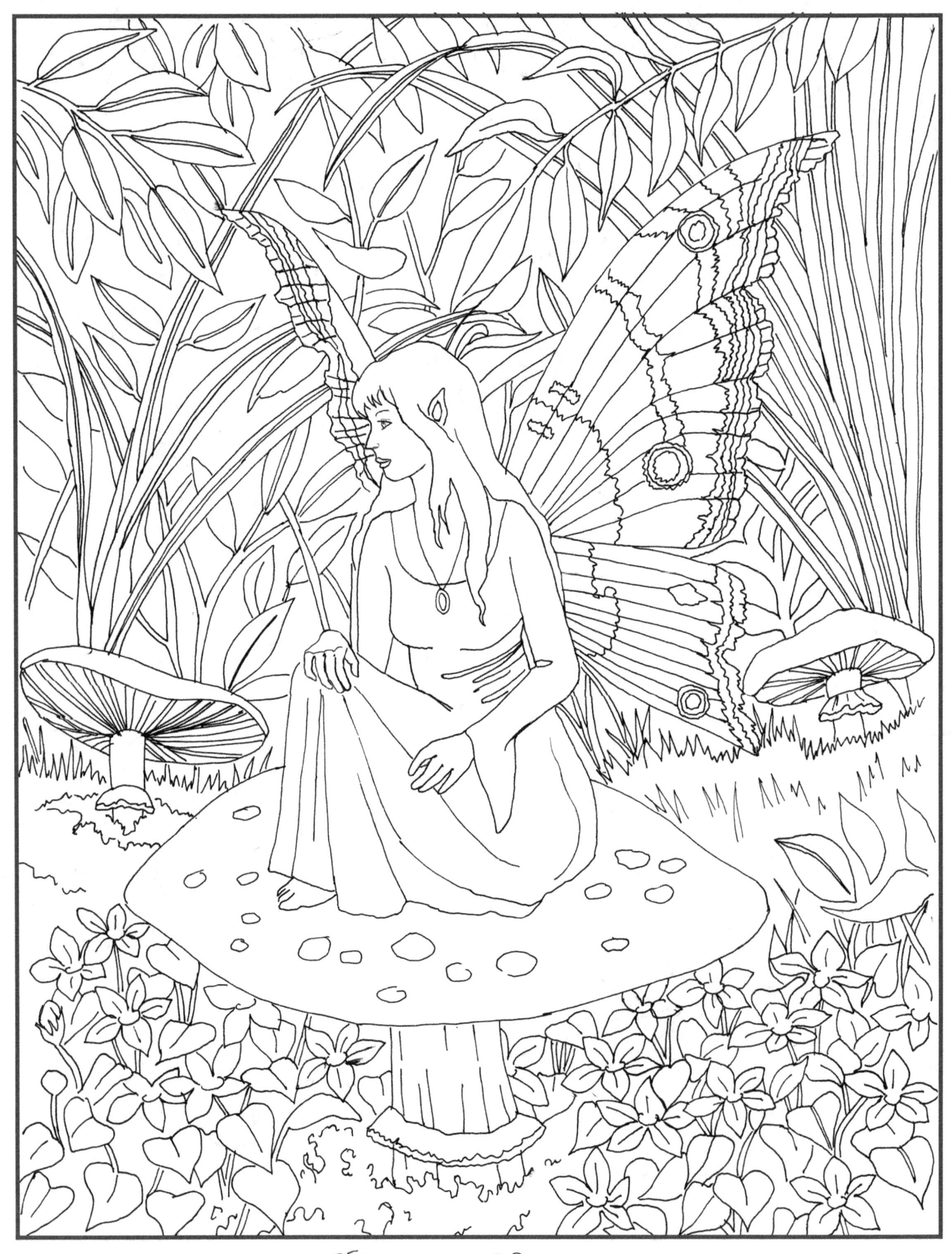

Forgotten Summer

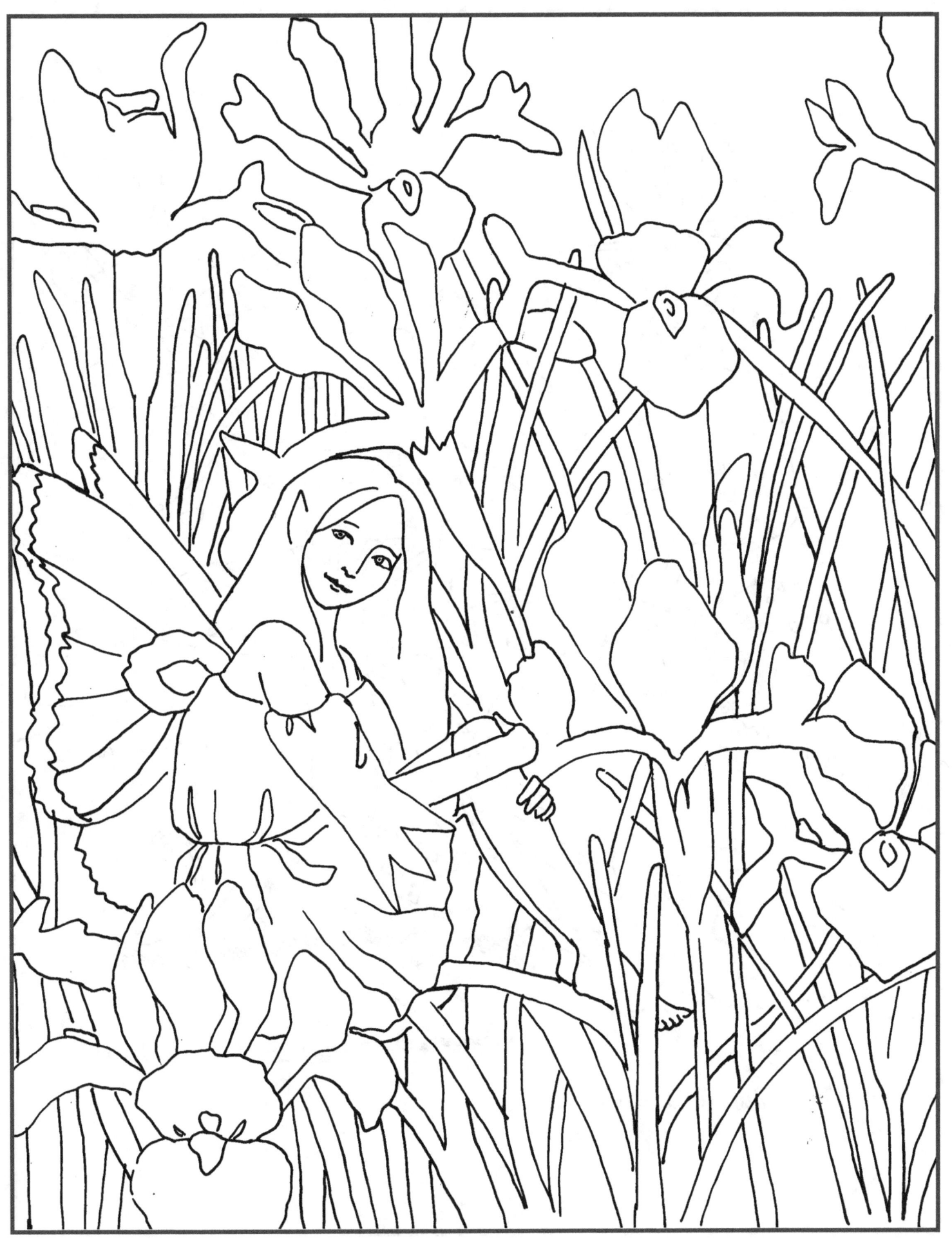

Iris

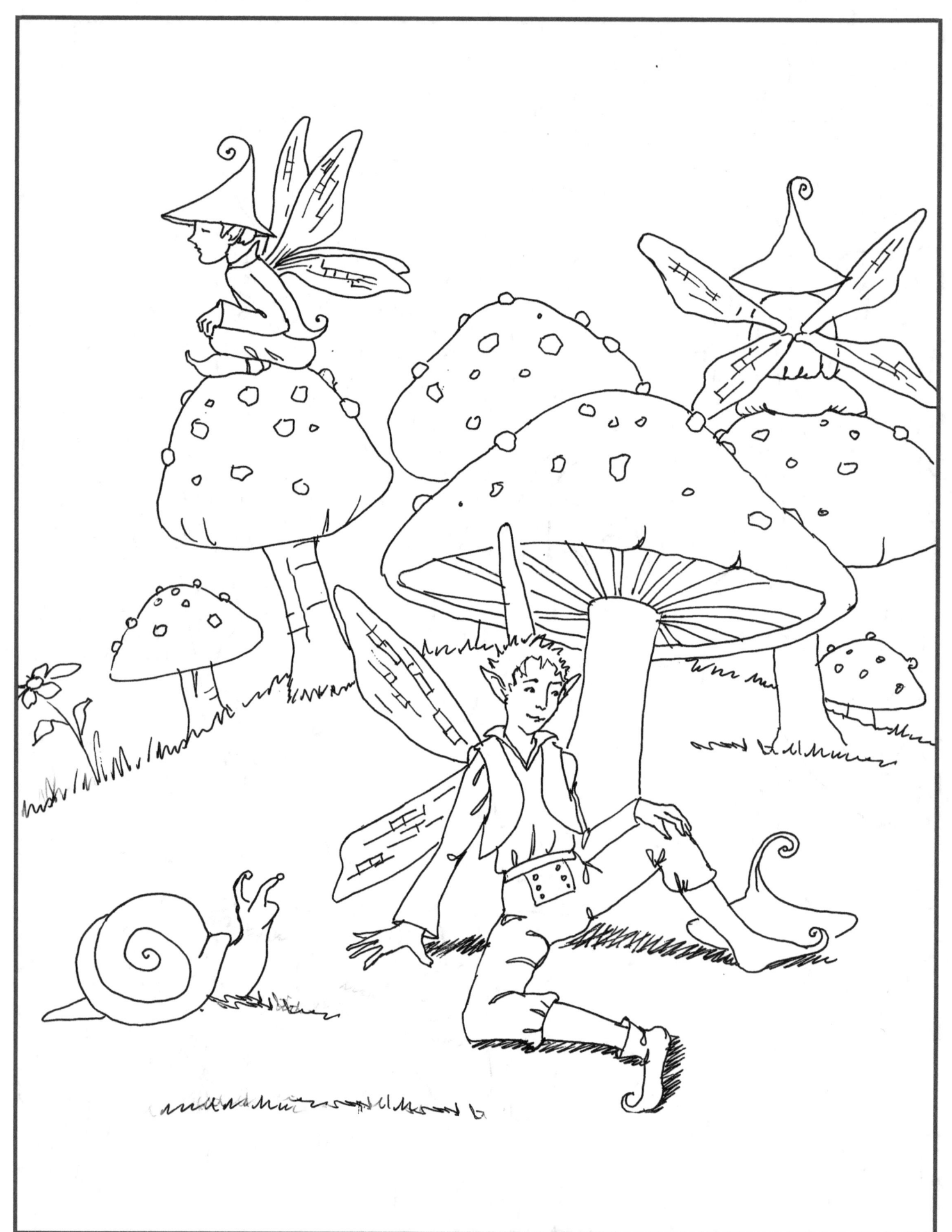

Great Thinkers

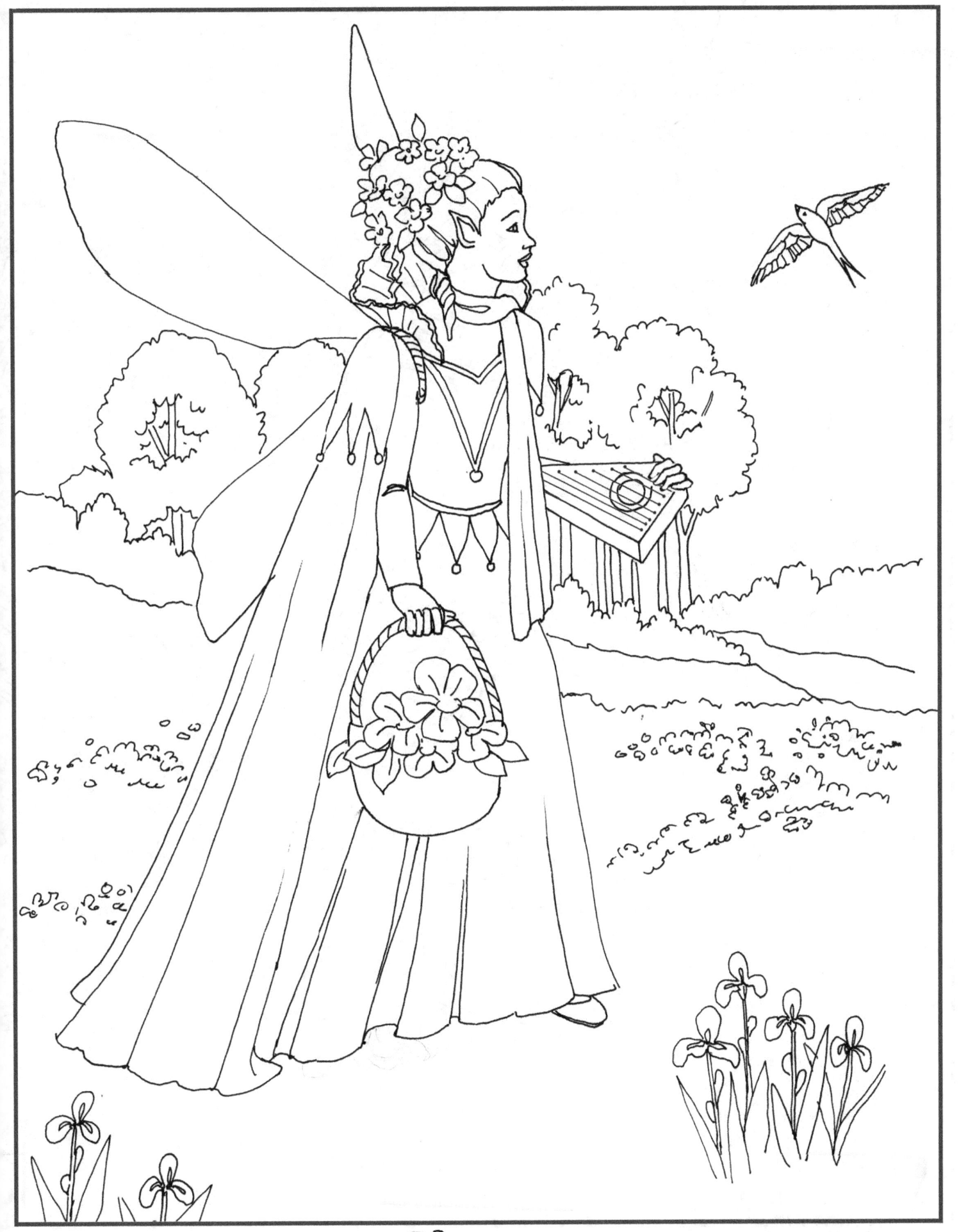

Meadowlark

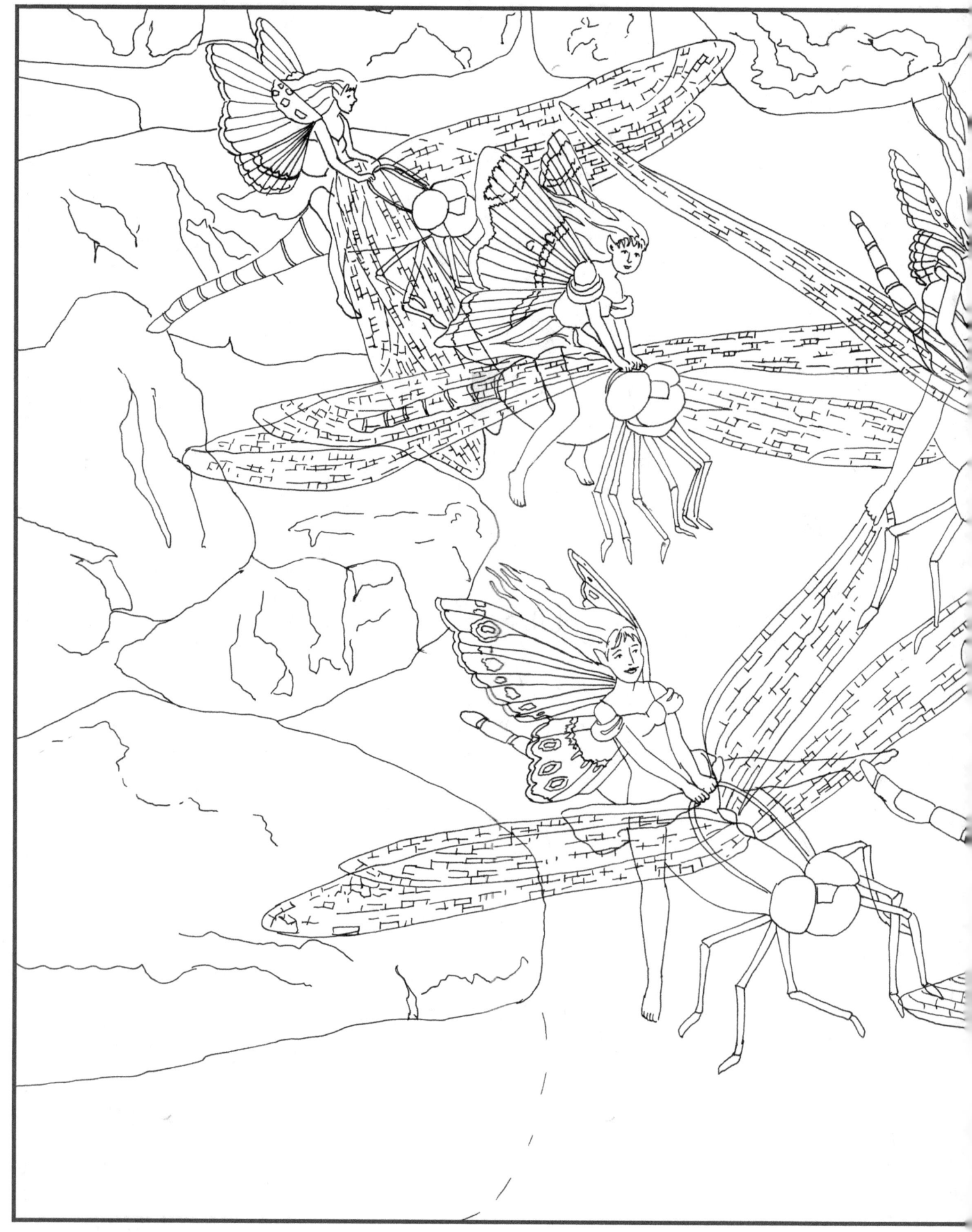

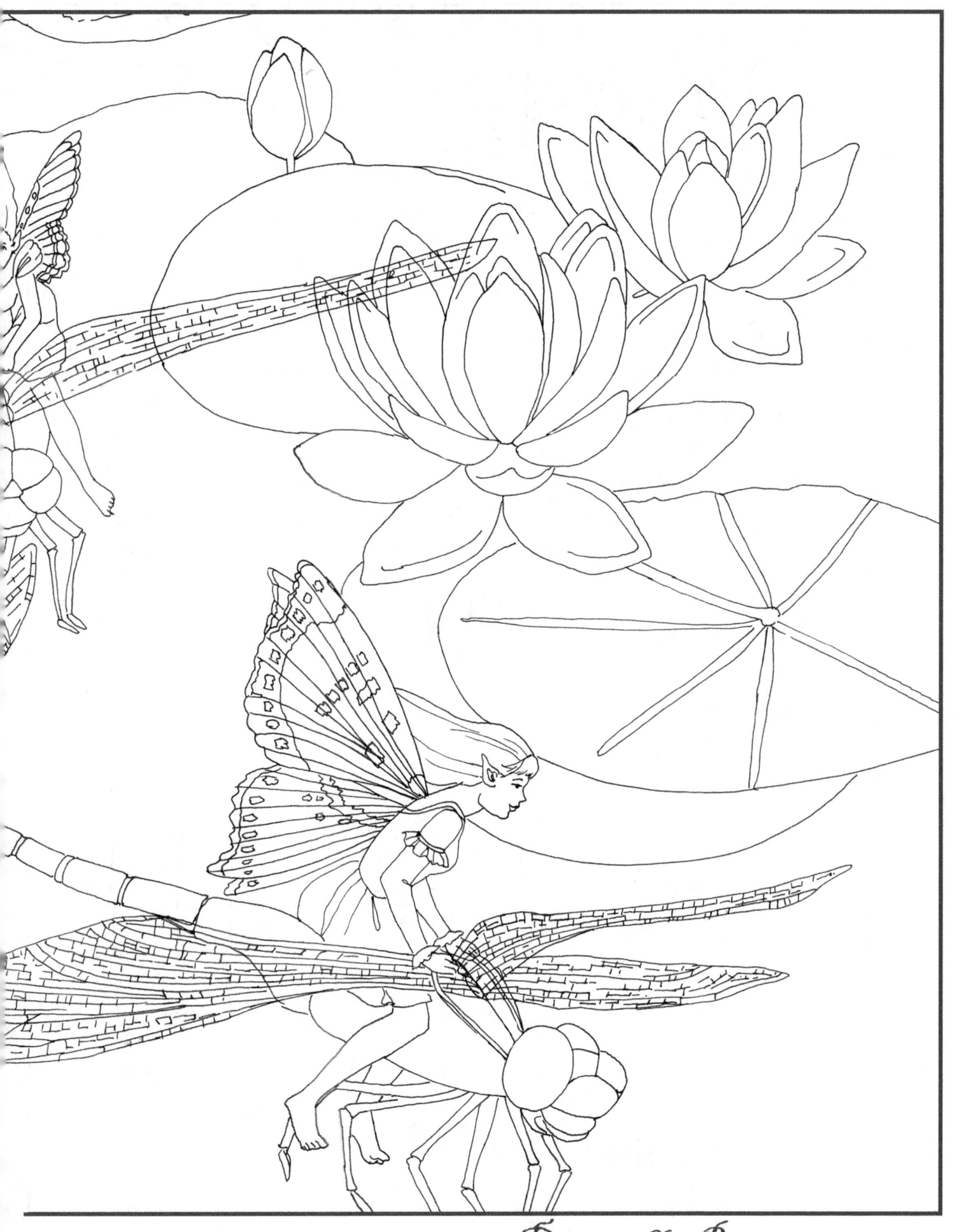

Dragonfly Race

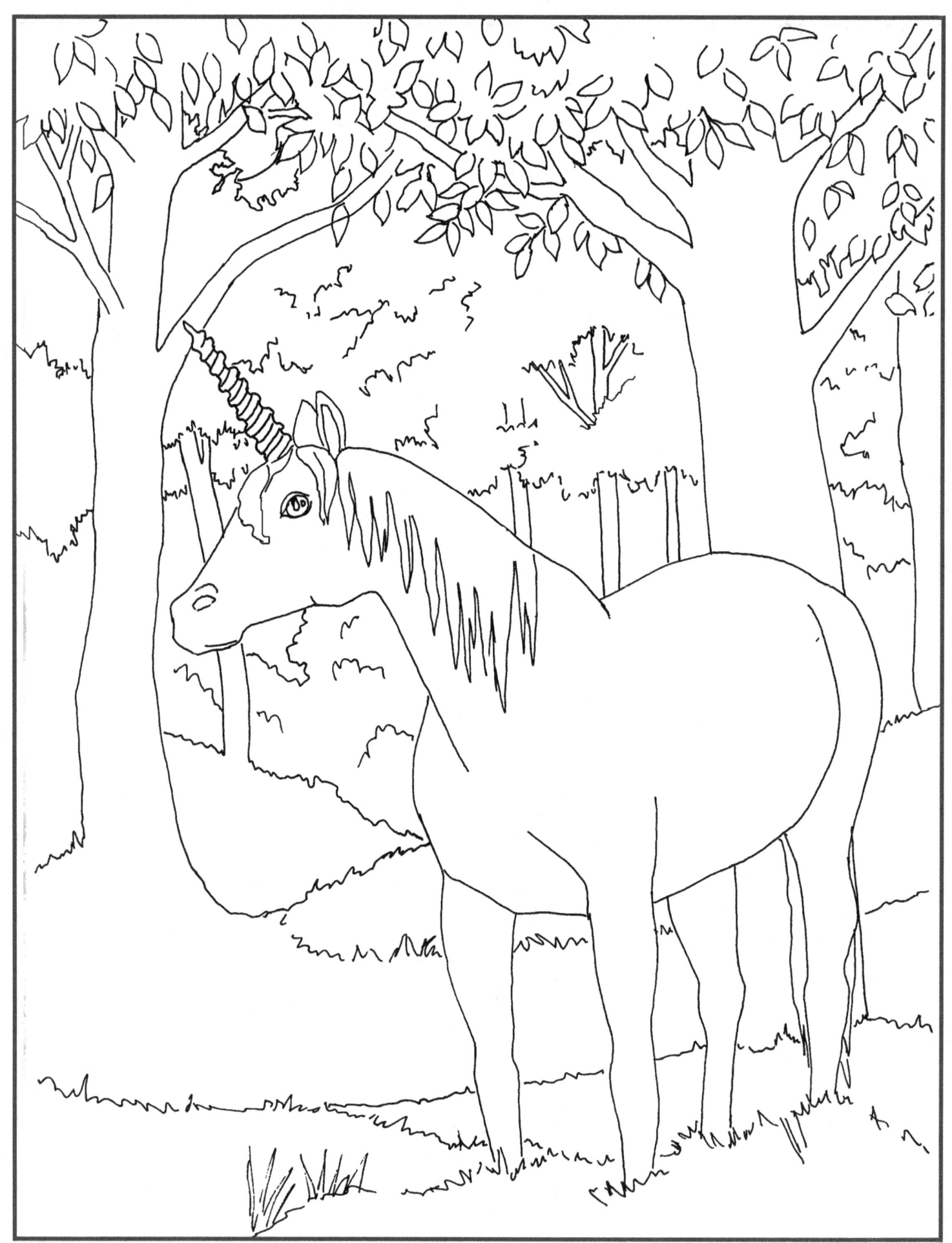

Moonlight

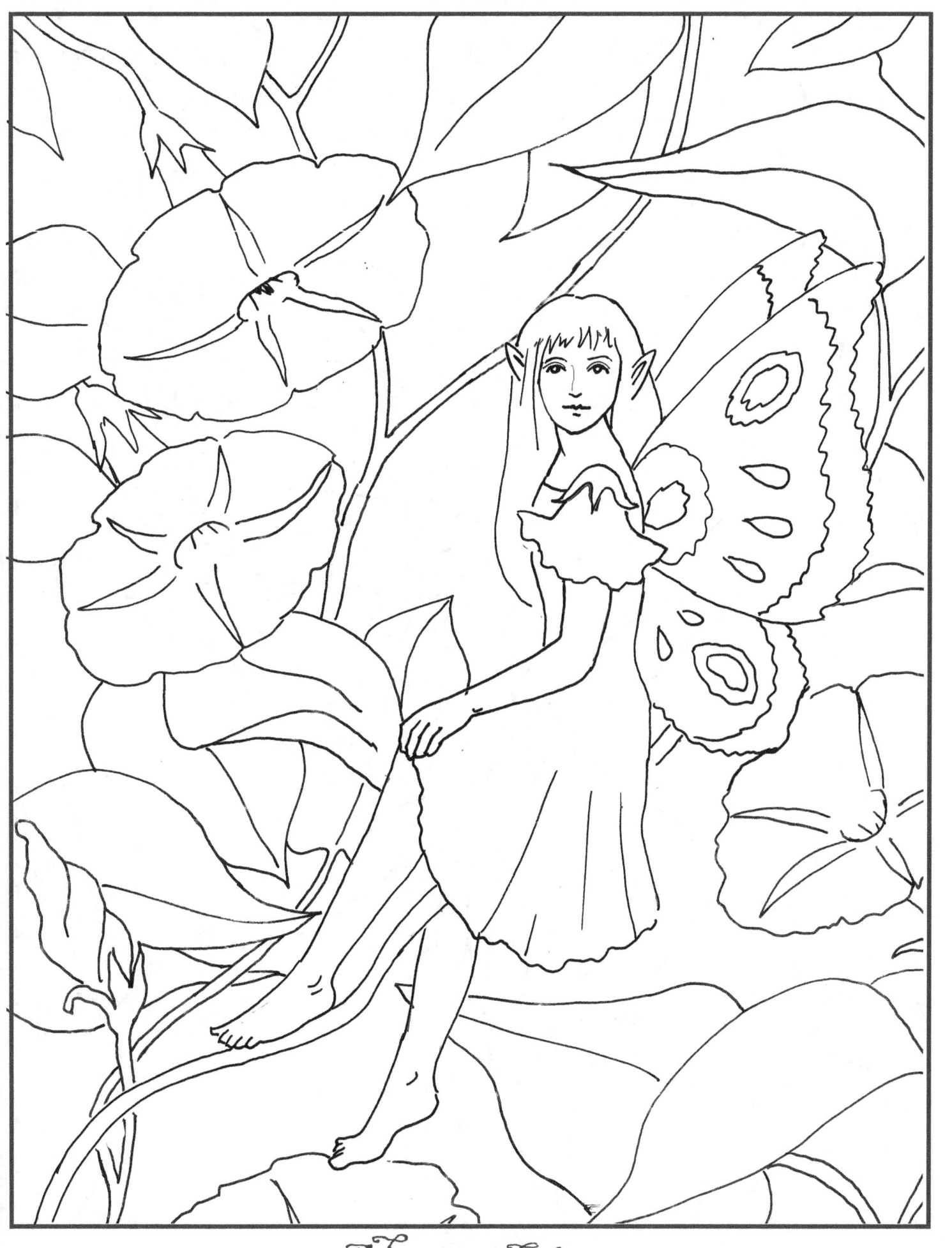

Morning Glory

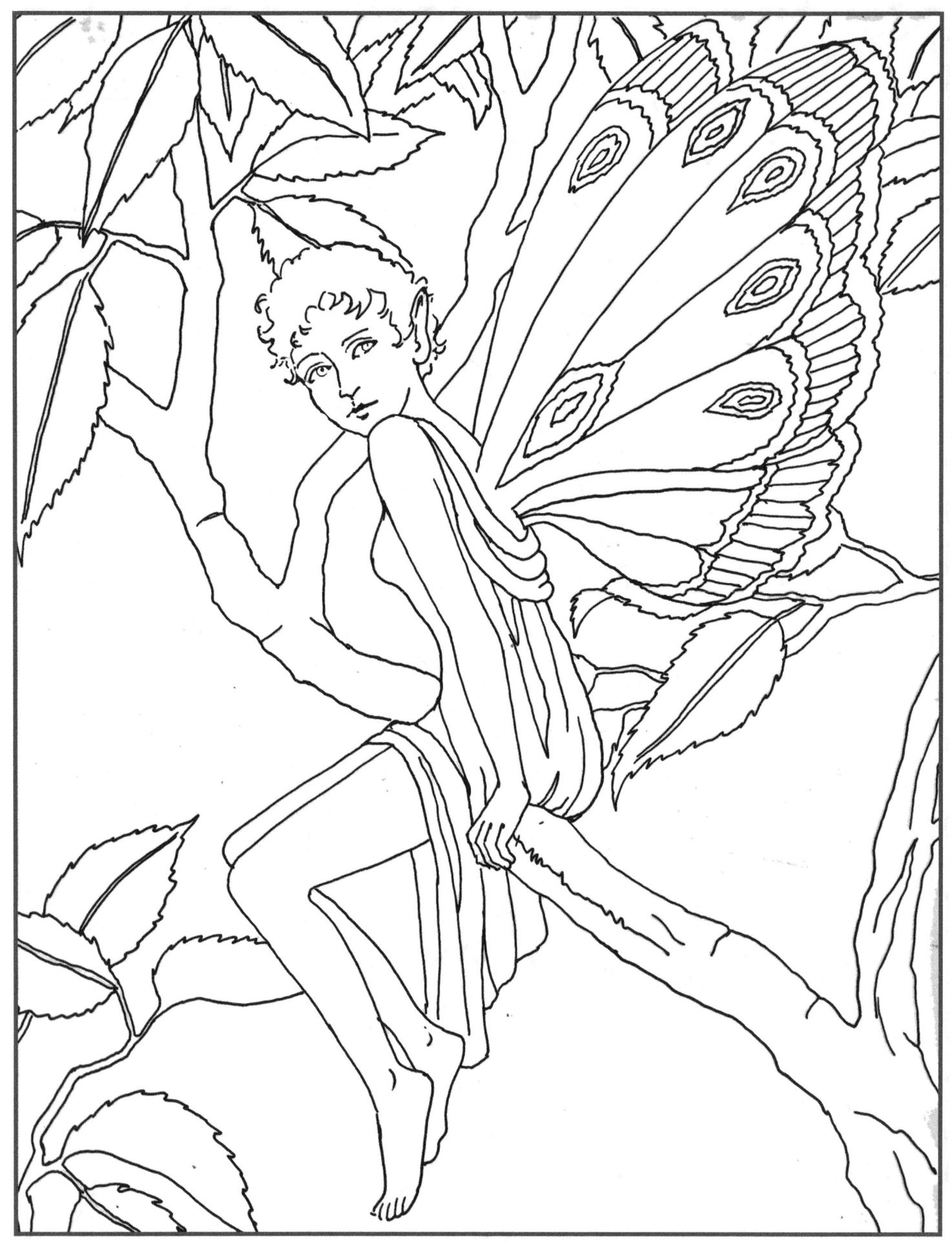

Unless

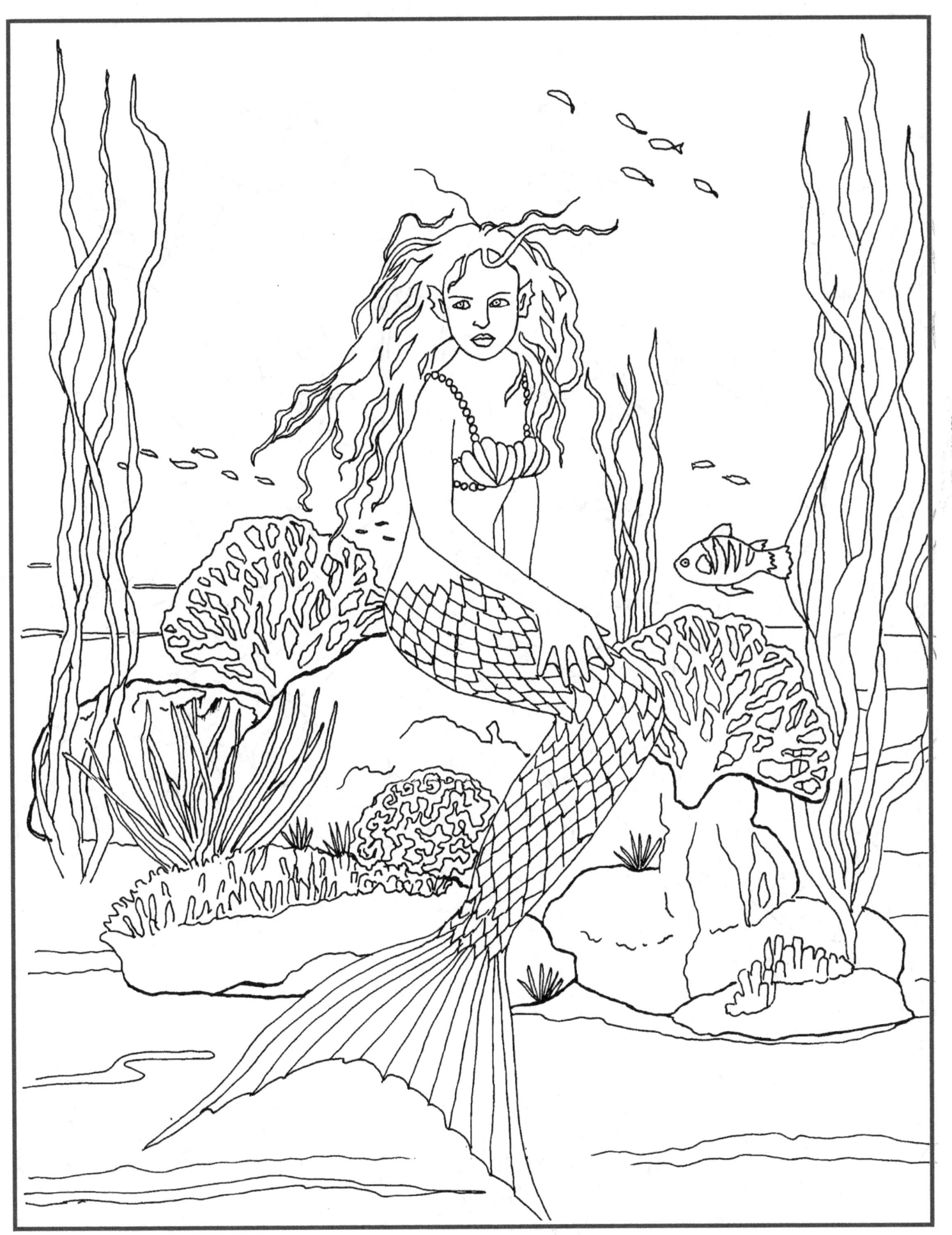

A Dark Current

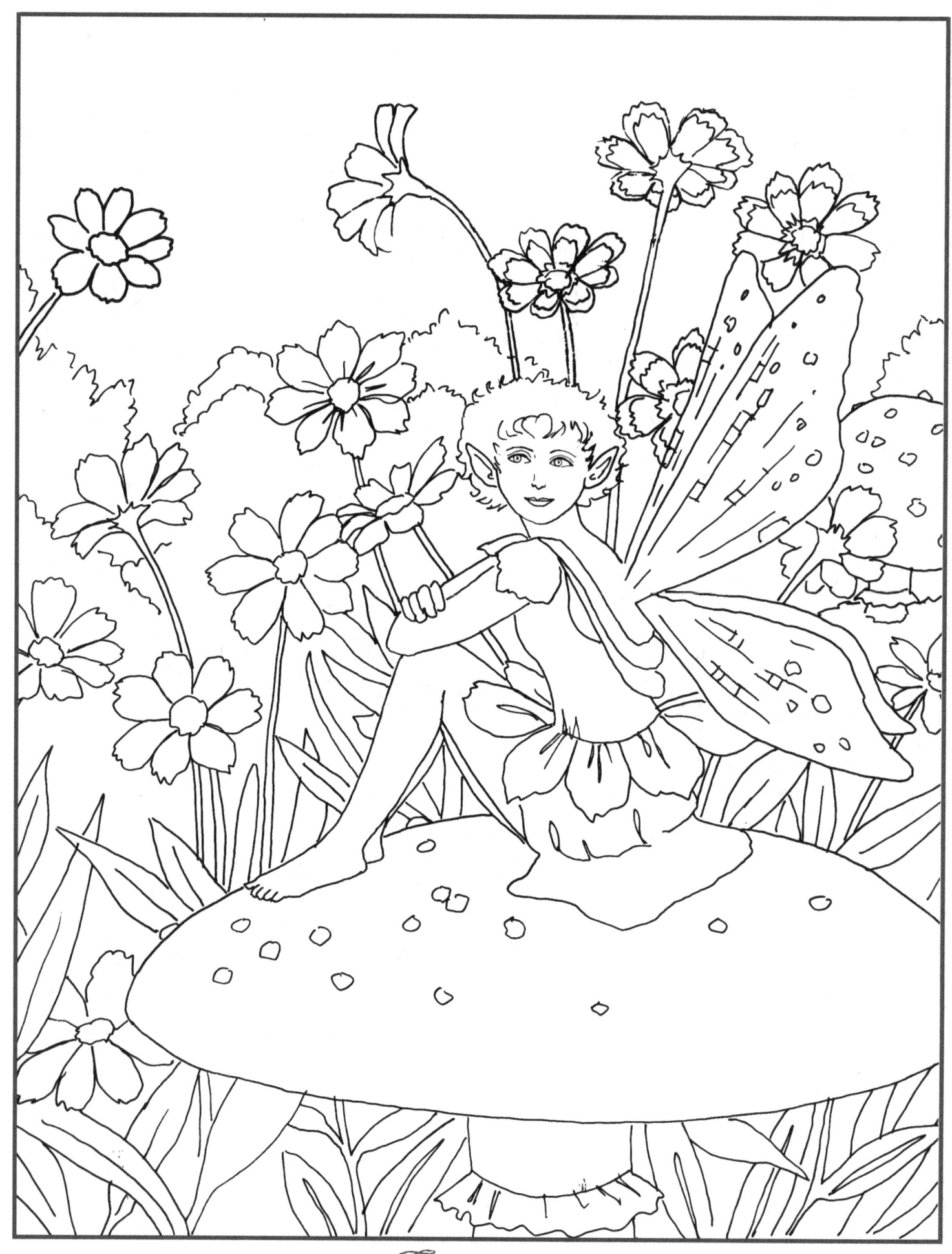

Coreopsis

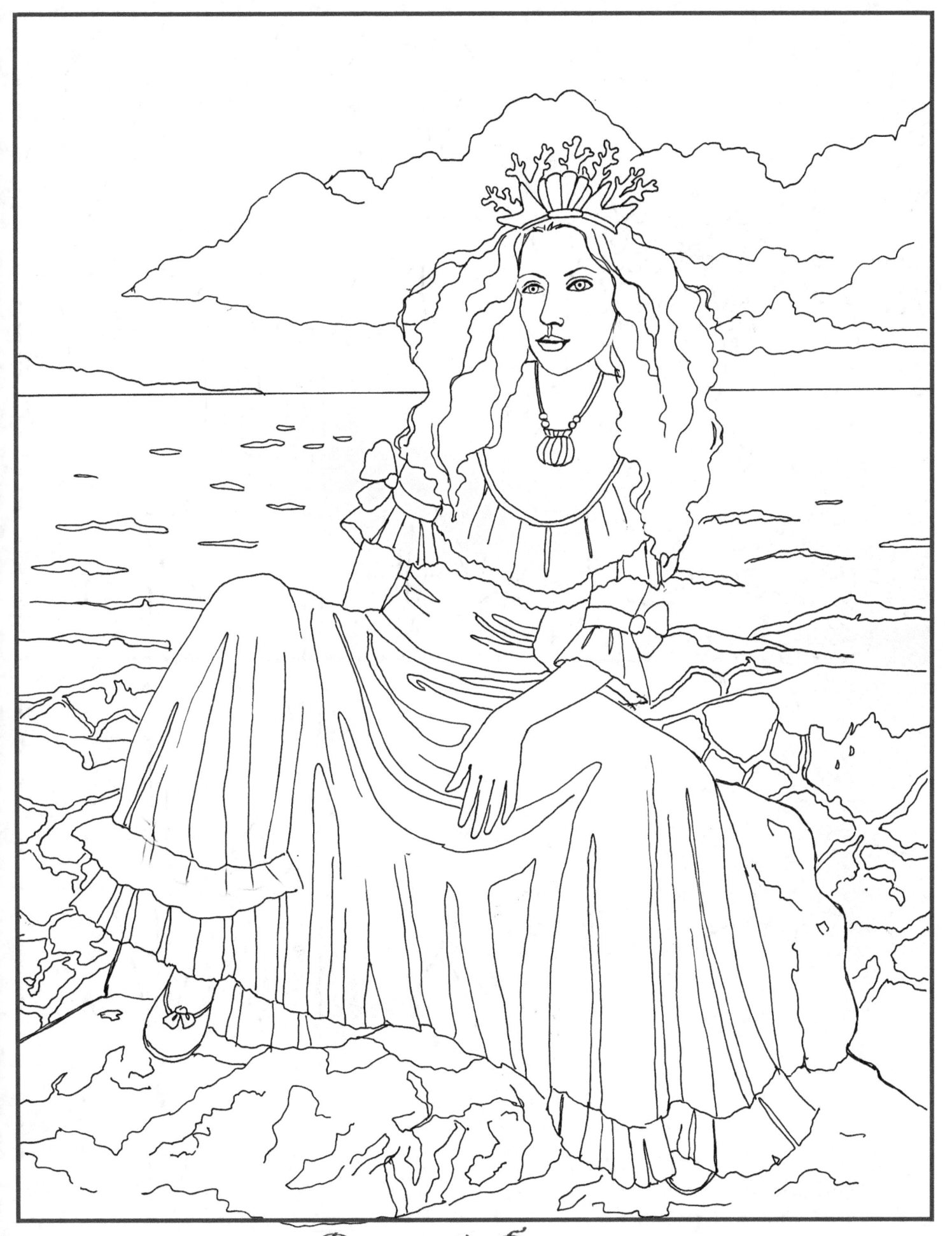

Poseidon's Daughter

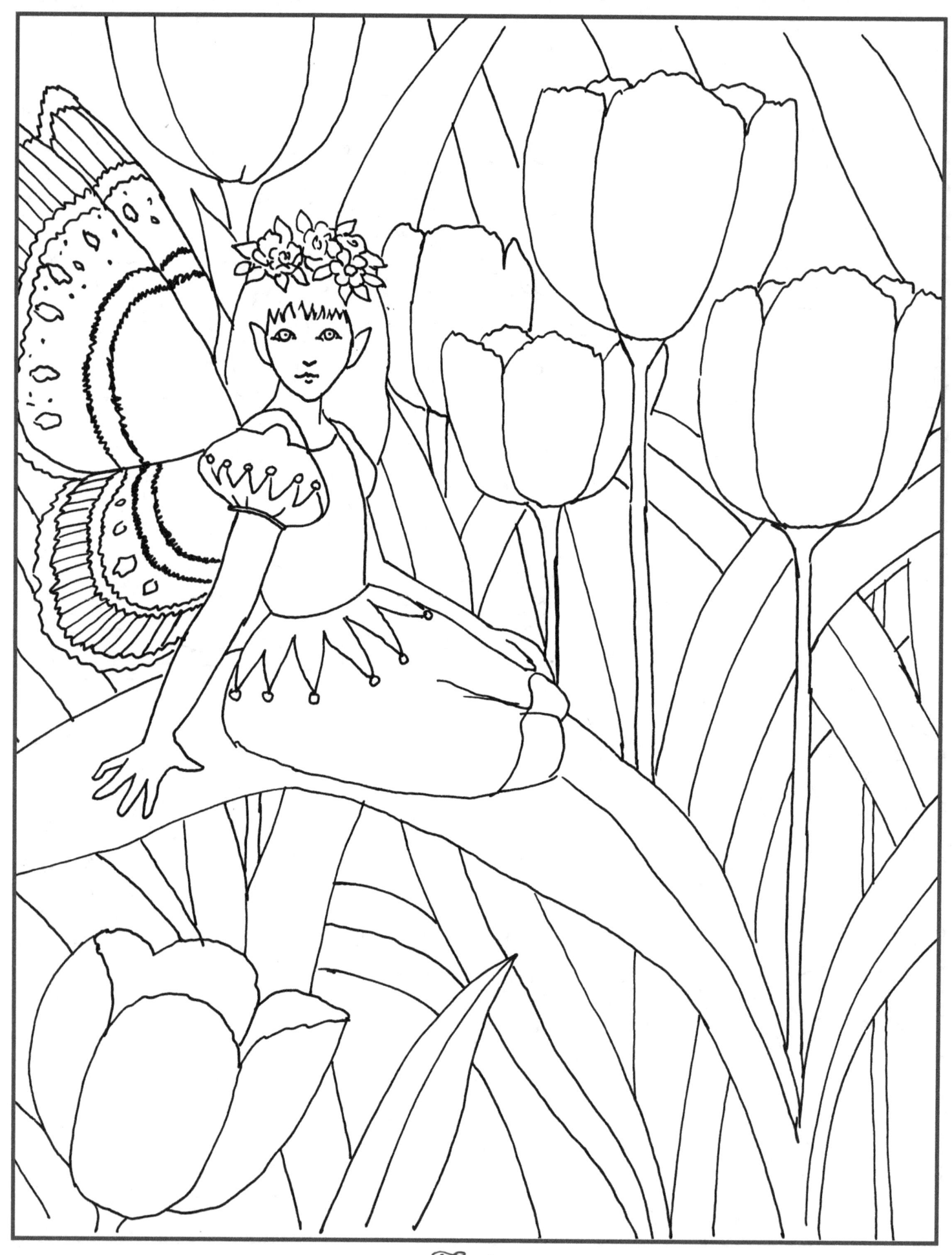

Tulip

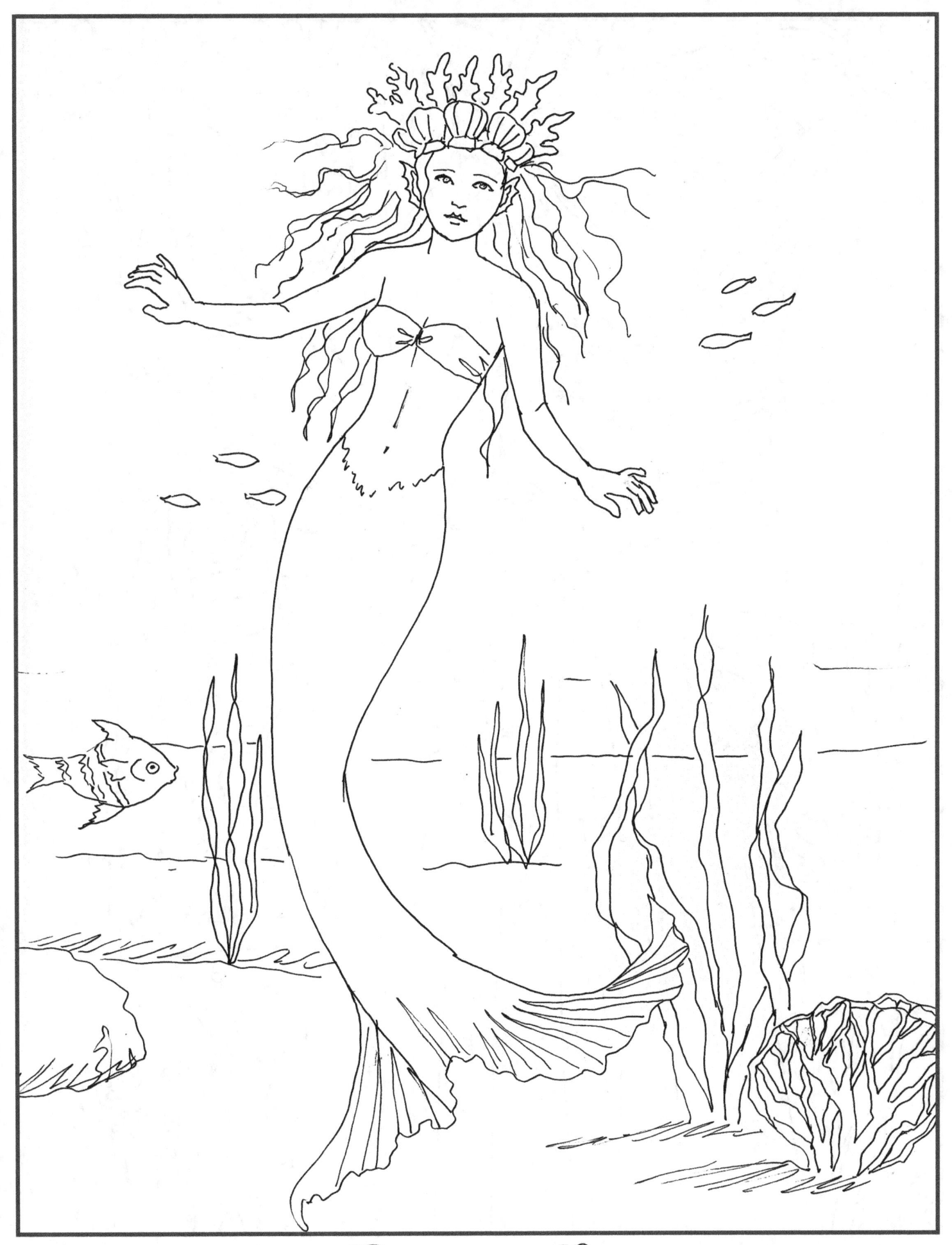

Queen of the Sea

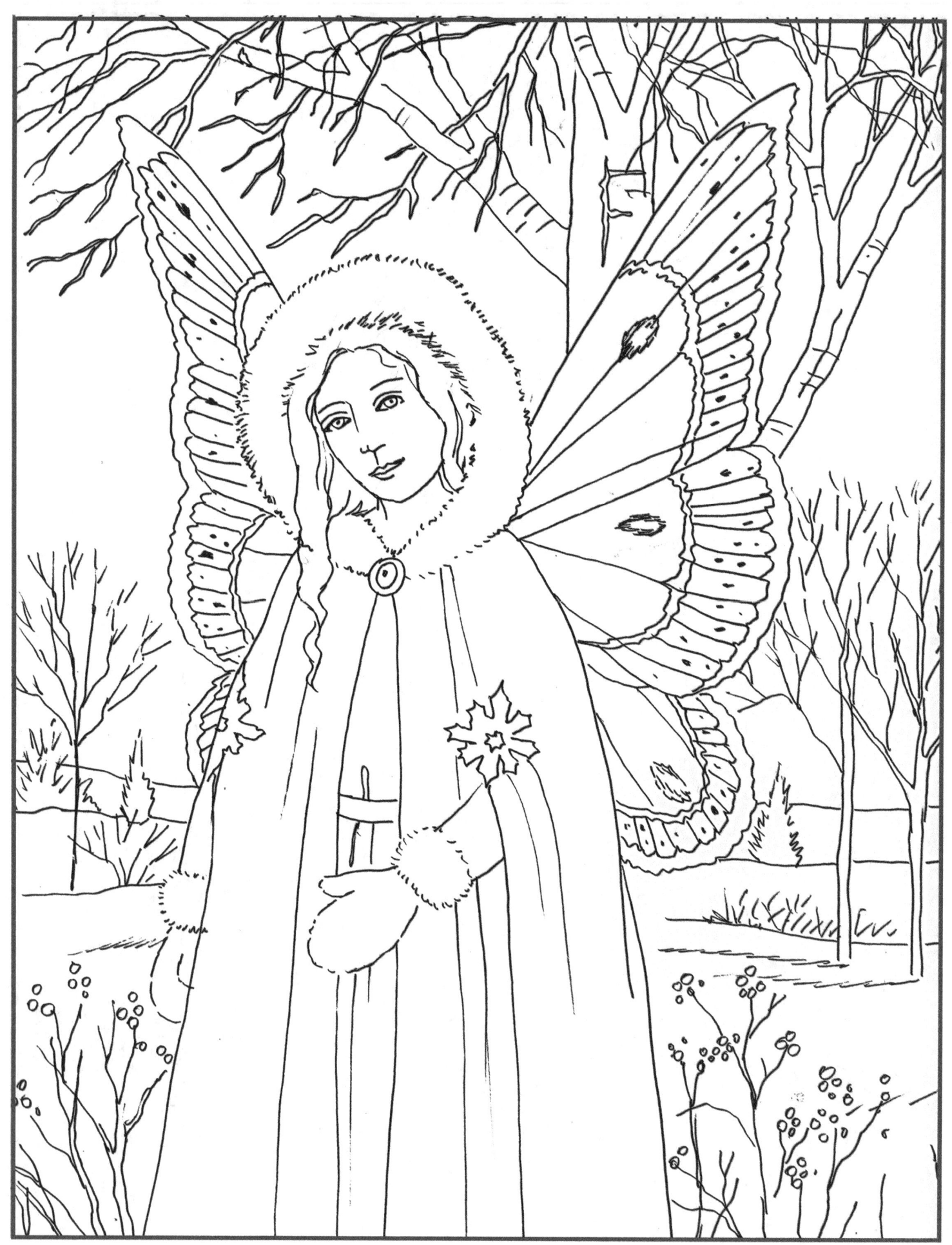

Snow Fairy

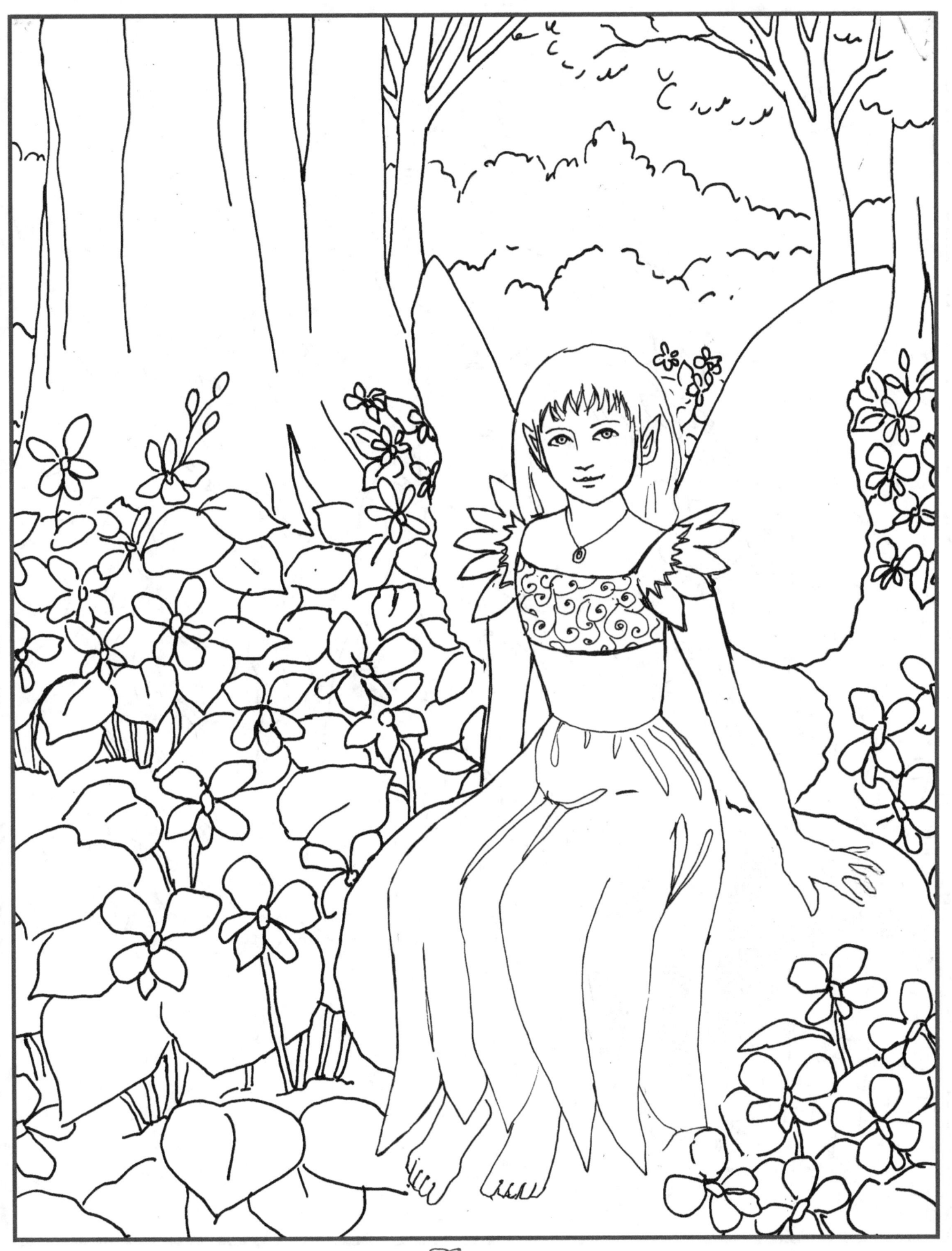

Violet

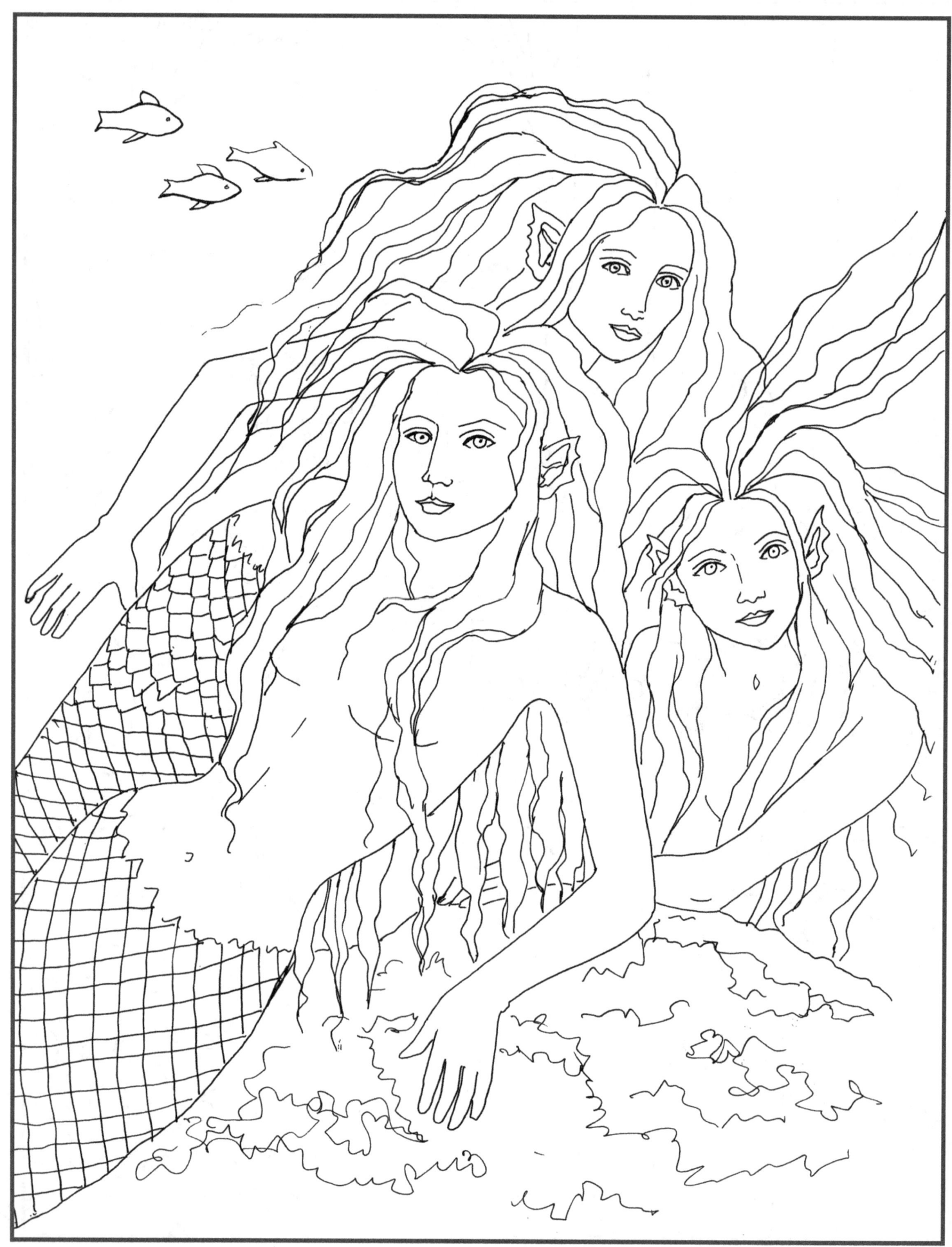

Sirens

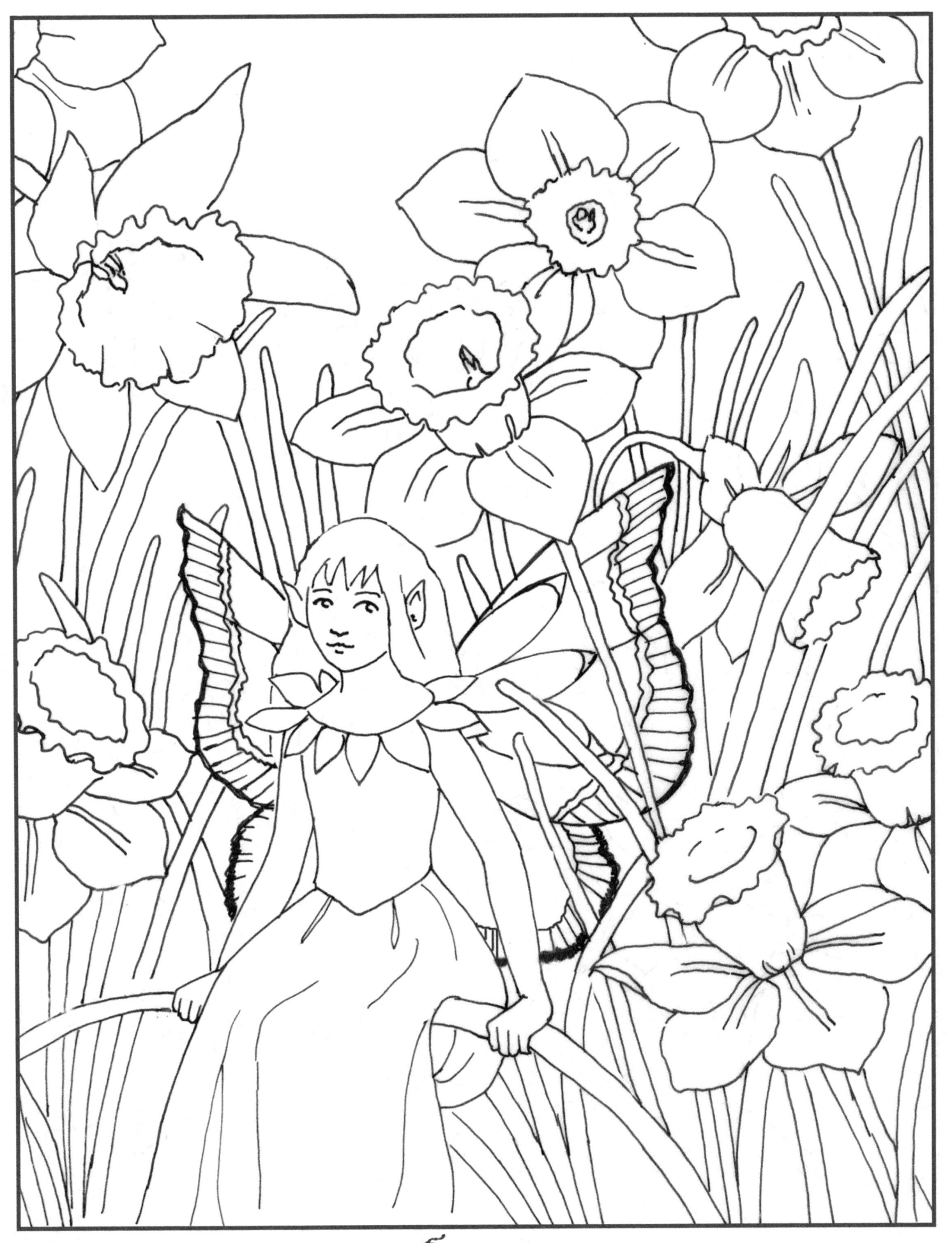

Daffodil

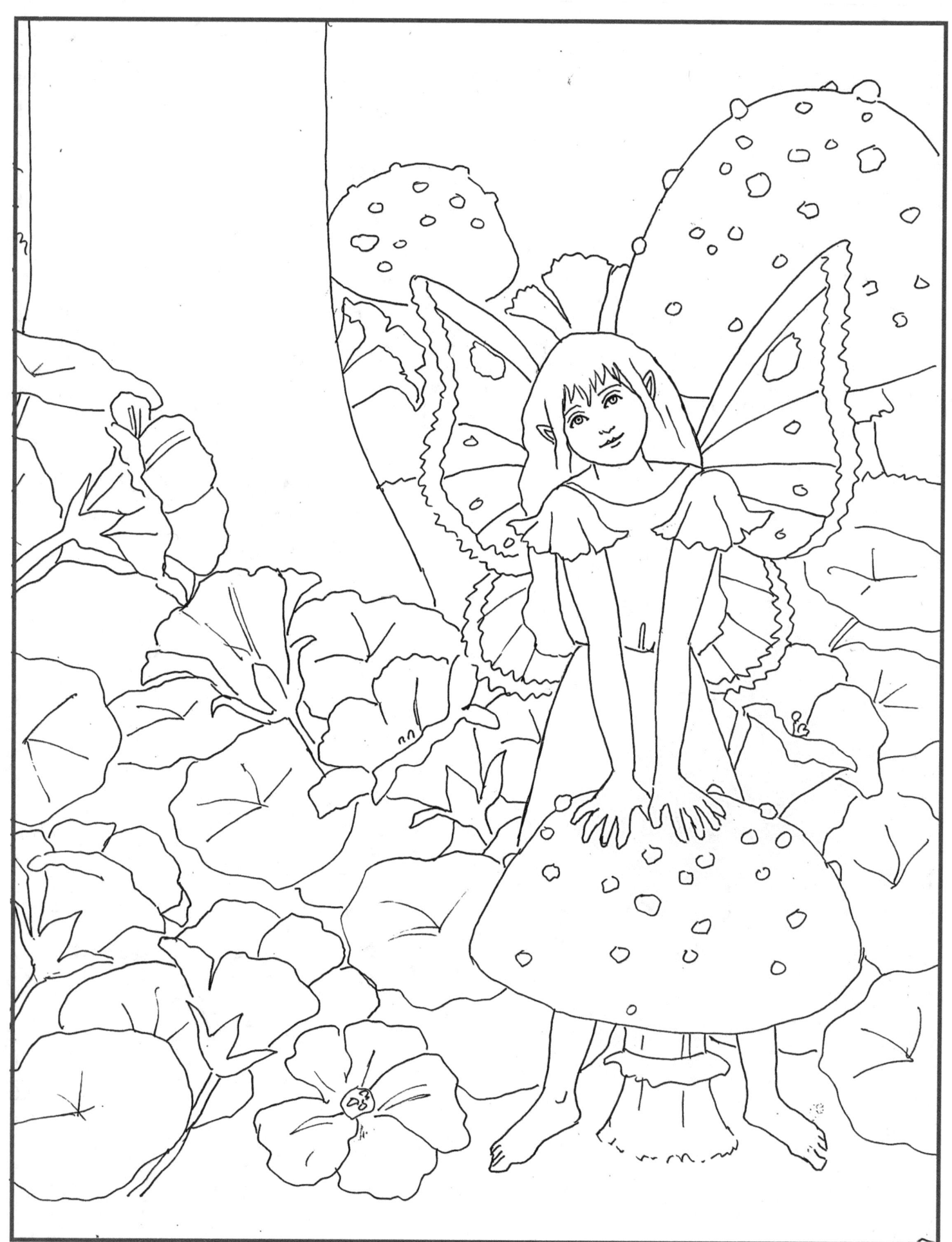

Nasturium

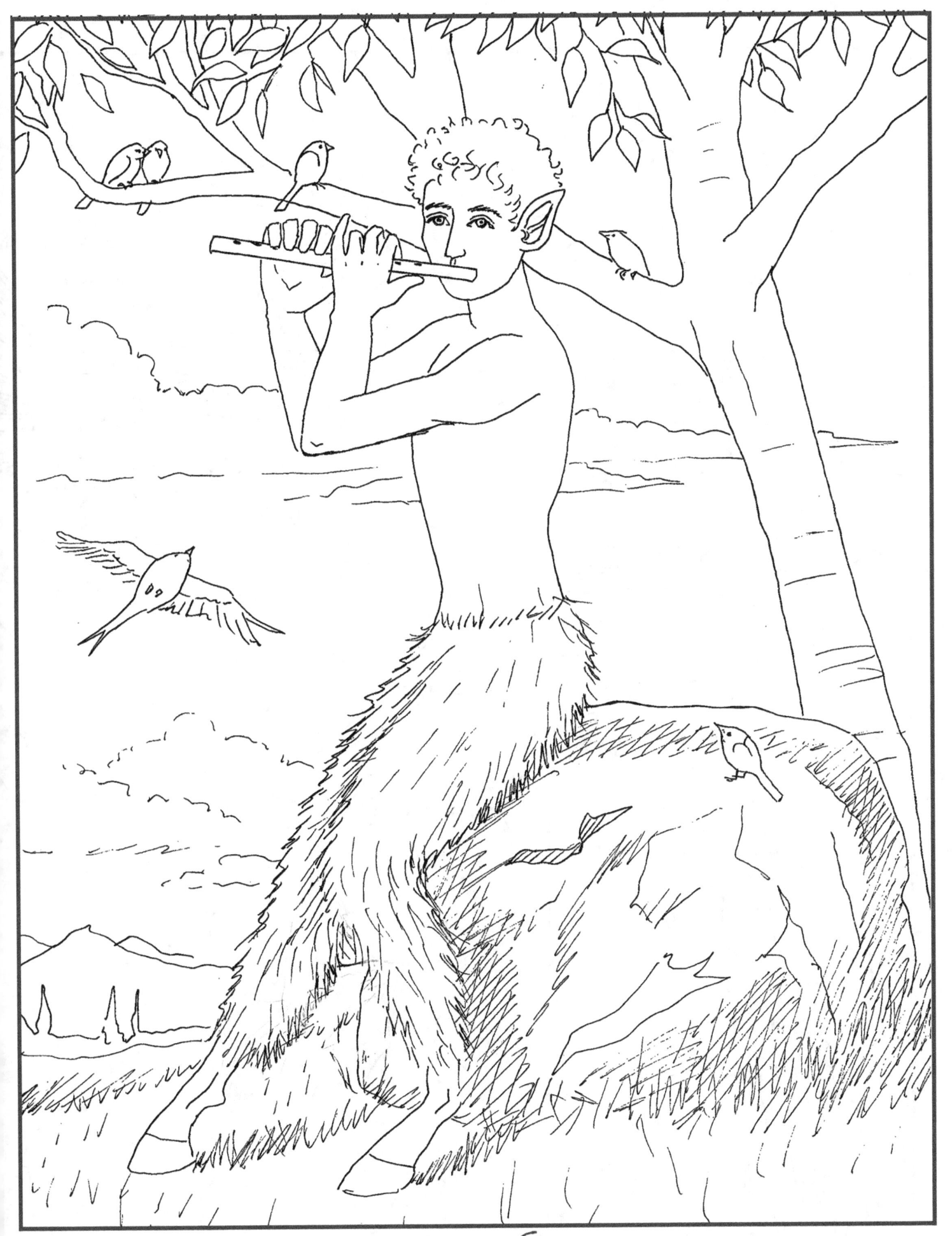

Satyr Pipe

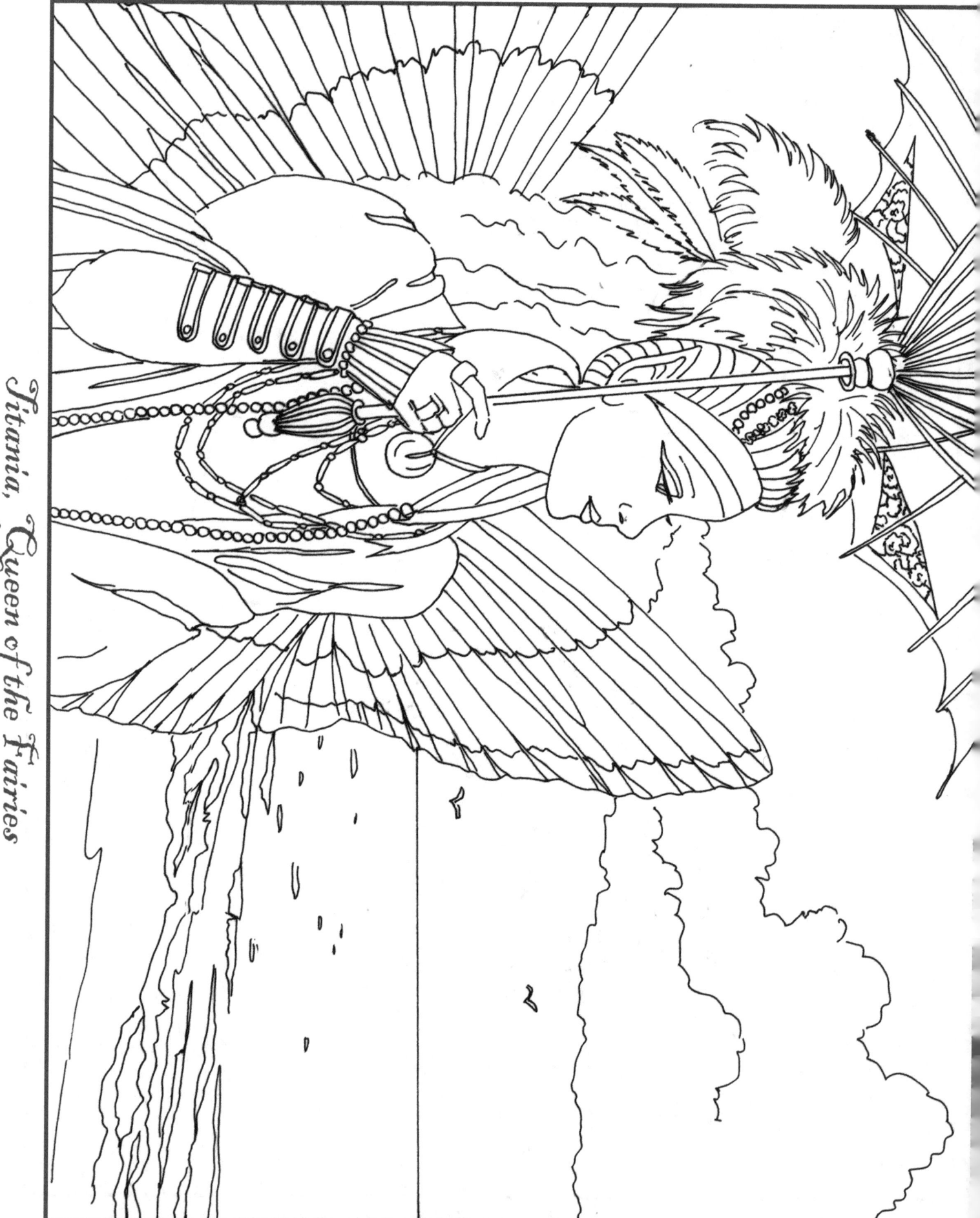

Titania, Queen of the Fairies

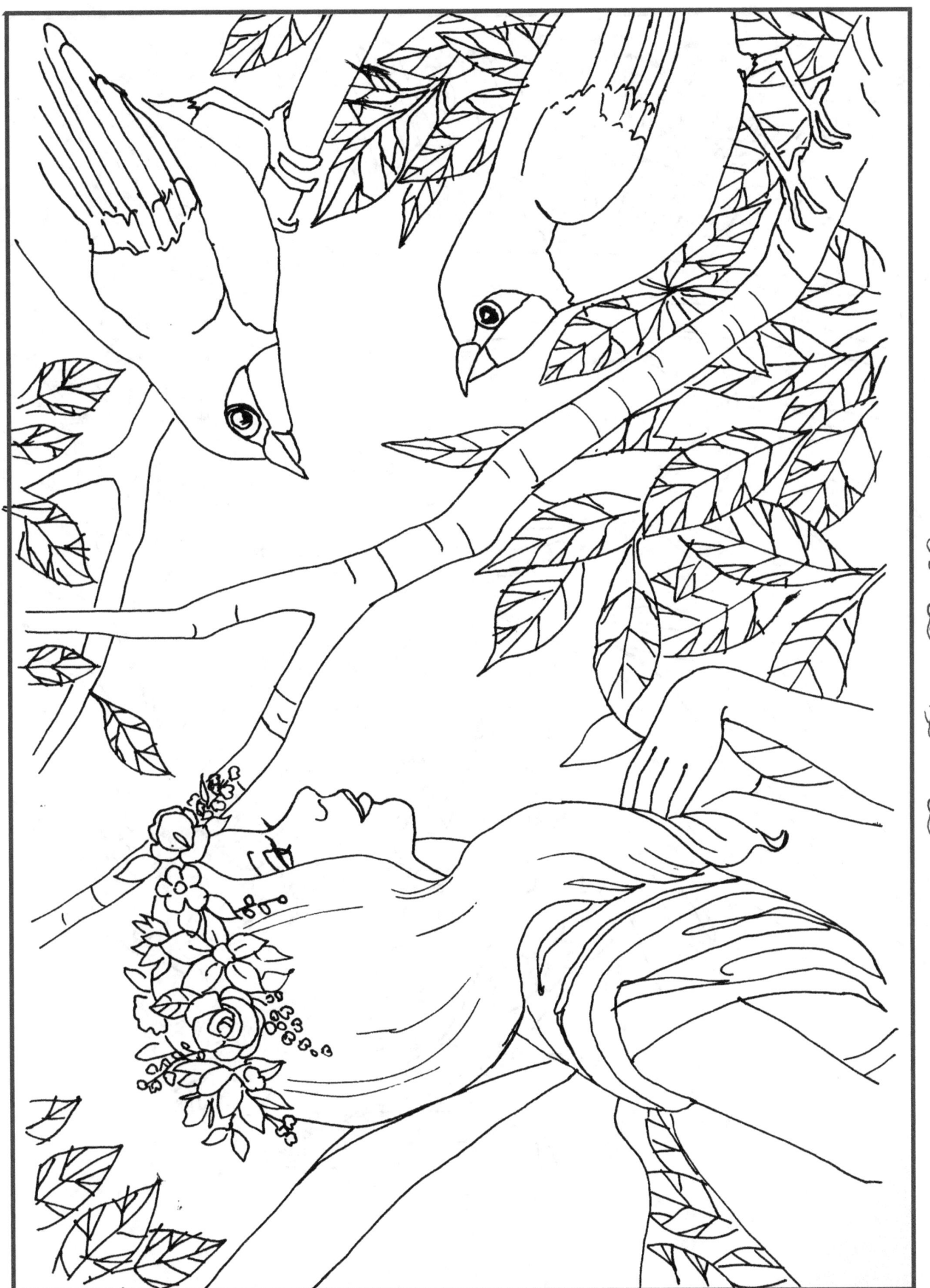

Tales From The South

Beauty

Dawn

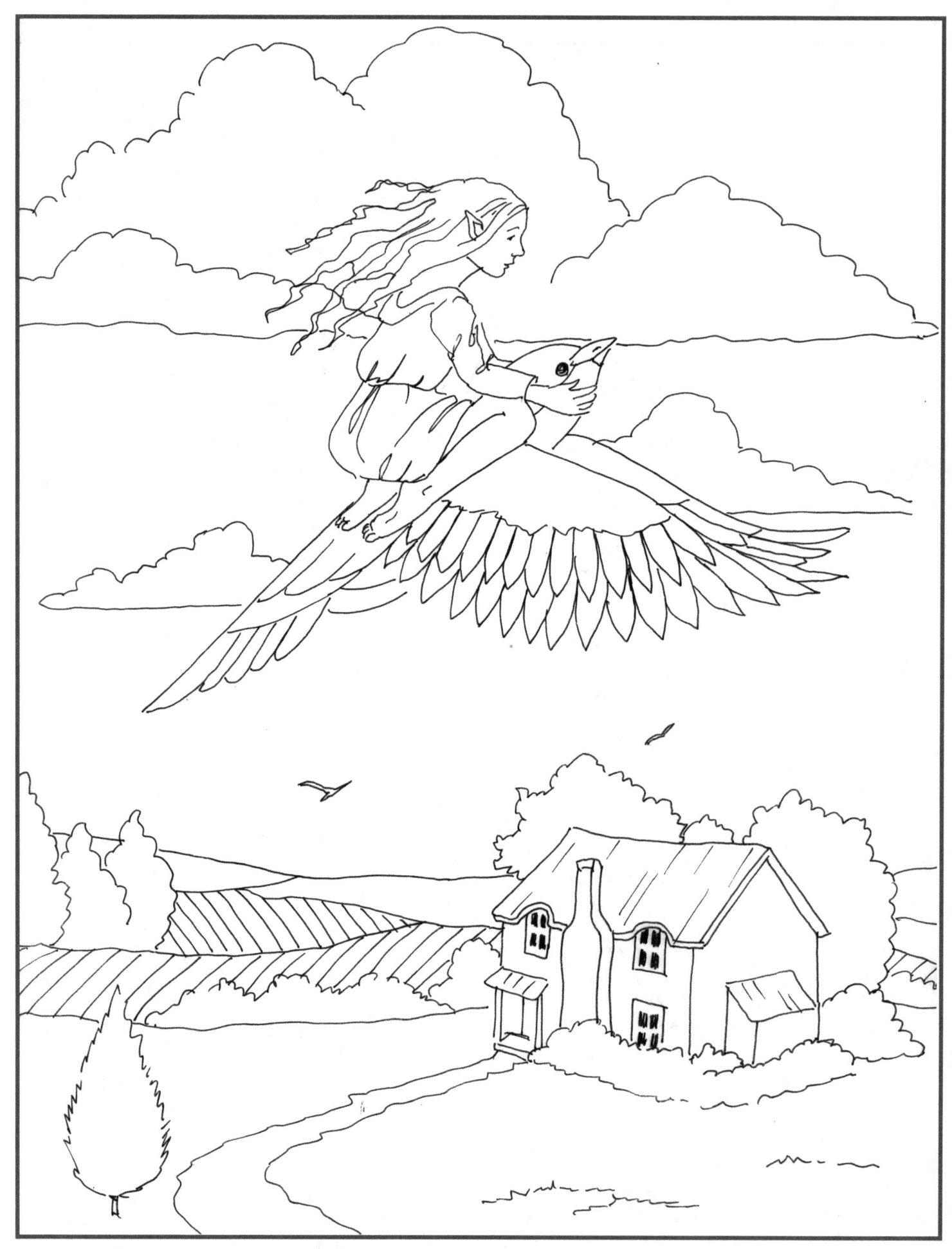

Flying With the Wind

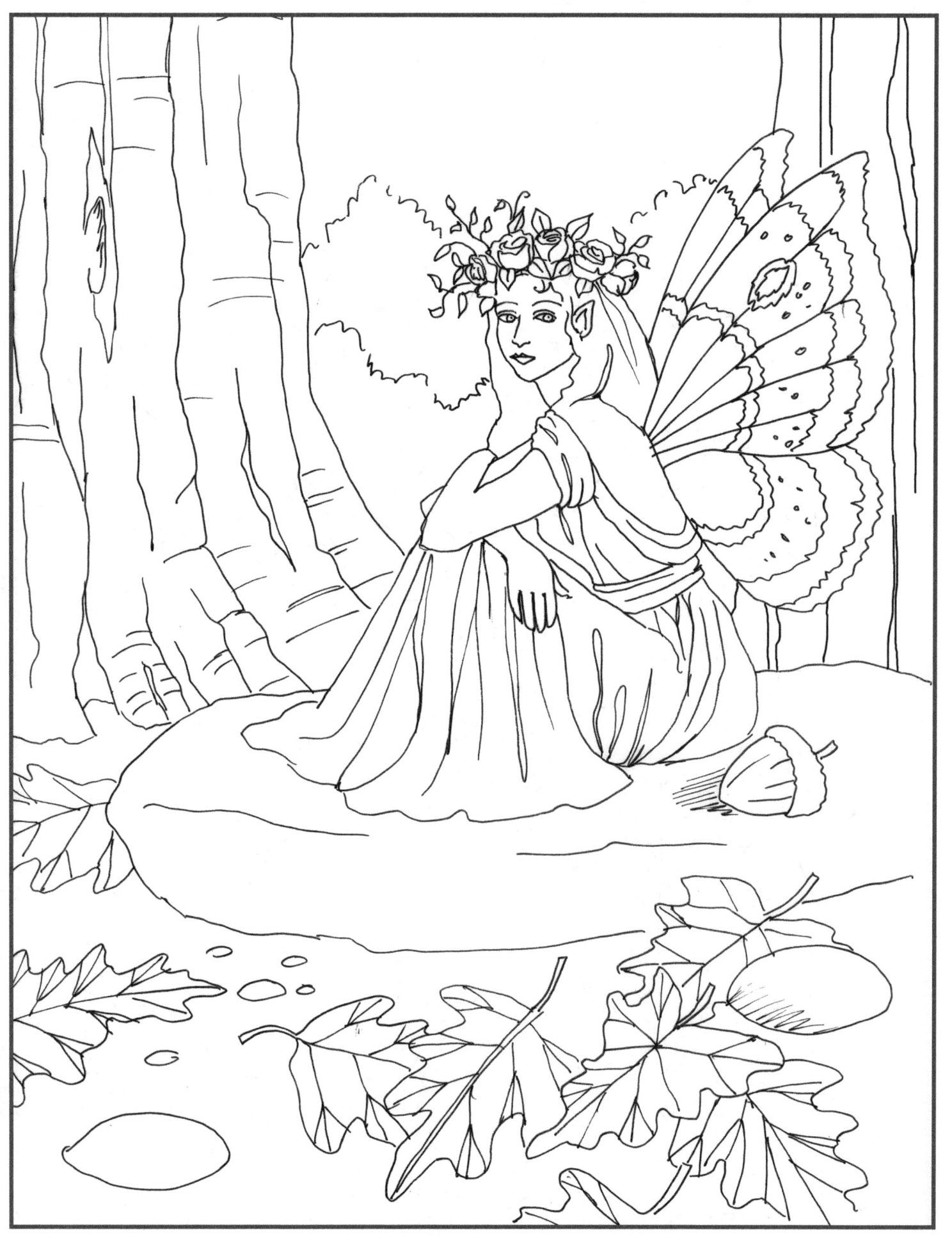

Autumn

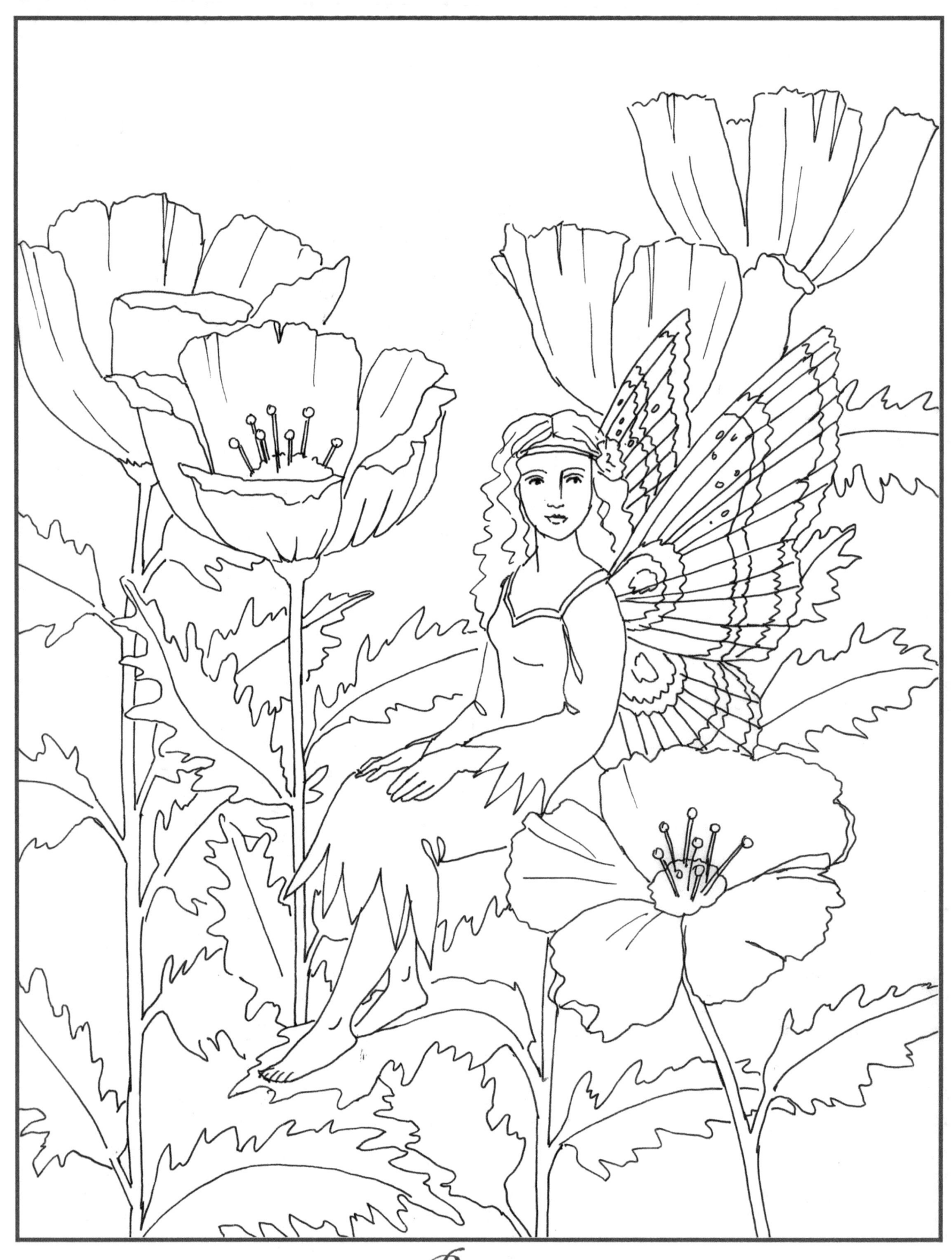

Poppy

The End